ALSO BY DAVID McCULLOUGH

The Pioneers
The American Spirit
The Wright Brothers
The Greater Journey
1776
John Adams
Truman
Brave Companions
Mornings on Horseback
The Path Between the Seas
The Great Bridge
The Johnstown Flood

HISTORY MATTERS

DAVID McCULLOUGH

Edited by Dorie McCullough Lawson
and Michael Hill

Foreword by Jon Meacham

SIMON & SCHUSTER
New York   London   Amsterdam/Antwerp
Toronto   Sydney/Melbourne   New Delhi

Simon and Schuster
1230 Avenue of the Americas
New York, NY 10020

For more than 100 years, Simon & Schuster has championed authors and the stories they create. By respecting the copyright of an author's intellectual property, you enable Simon & Schuster and the author to continue publishing exceptional books for years to come. We thank you for supporting the author's copyright by purchasing an authorized edition of this book.

No amount of this book may be reproduced or stored in any format, nor may it be uploaded to any website, database, language-learning model, or other repository, retrieval, or artificial intelligence system without express permission. All rights reserved. Inquiries may be directed to Simon & Schuster, 1230 Avenue of the Americas, New York, NY 10020 or permissions@simonandschuster.com.

Copyright © 2025 by Music Street, LLC

Foreword © Jon Meacham, adapted from "Rethinking Washington," *Newsweek*, May 22, 2005

David McCullough, "The Art of Biography No. 2," interviewed by Elizabeth Gaffney and Benjamin Ryder Howe, was first published in *The Paris Review*. Copyright © 1999 by The Paris Review Foundation, Inc., used by permission of The Wylie Agency, LLC.

The essay "Harriet Beecher Stowe in Paris" was originally published in the August 2011 issue of *American History Magazine* with the title "The Little Woman Who Started a Big War."

Title page photo: Alison Shaw

Front endpaper: watercolor by David McCullough of the McCullough house in West Tisbury, Massachusetts

Back endpaper: watercolor by David McCullough of his office and yard at the house in West Tisbury, Massachusetts

All rights reserved, including the right to reproduce this book or portions thereof in any form whatsoever. For information, address Simon & Schuster Subsidiary Rights Department, 1230 Avenue of the Americas, New York, NY 10020.

First Simon & Schuster hardcover edition September 2025

SIMON & SCHUSTER and colophon are registered trademarks of Simon & Schuster, LLC

Simon & Schuster strongly believes in freedom of expression and stands against censorship in all its forms. For more information, visit BooksBelong.com.

For information about special discounts for bulk purchases, please contact Simon & Schuster Special Sales at 1-866-506-1949 or business@simonandschuster.com.

The Simon & Schuster Speakers Bureau can bring authors to your live event. For more information or to book an event, contact the Simon & Schuster Speakers Bureau at 1-866-248-3049 or visit our website at www.simonspeakers.com.

Interior design by Wendy Blum

Manufactured in the United States of America

10 9 8 7 6 5 4 3 2 1

Library of Congress Cataloging-in-Publication data is available.

ISBN 978-1-6680-9899-8
ISBN 978-1-6680-9901-8 (ebook)

CONTENTS

Preface by Dorie McCullough Lawson	ix
Foreword by Jon Meacham	xi

PART ONE: WHY HISTORY?

Why History?	3
American Values	7
Take Luck to Heart	17
The Good Work of America	23
"The Art of Biography," *The Paris Review* Interview	27

PART TWO: FIGURES IN A LANDSCAPE

Thomas Eakins	51
Harriet Beecher Stowe in Paris	59
A Conversation About George	67
Harry S. Truman	77

PART THREE: INFLUENCES

The Love of Learning	99
Tribute to Vincent Scully	111
Getting Through to Schlesinger	115
Tribute to Paul Horgan	121
Accuracy and Imagination: Tribute to Herman Wouk	131
Favorite and Influential Books	137
A Book on Every Bed	141

PART FOUR: ON WRITING

The Good, Hard Work of Writing Well	145
A Bit of History About My Typewriter	151
Reading and Writing: A Recommended Reading List	155
History and Art	165

About the Authors	169

PREFACE

Dorie McCullough Lawson

I began working with my father in 1992, just after the publication of *Truman*. At the time, the head of publicity at Simon & Schuster was Victoria Meyer. Victoria was seasoned and direct, and she knew what she was doing. She recognized right away that we were running into a language problem between us: When we were working, talking about our main subject, David McCullough, what should we call him? She didn't want to say "your father," but calling him David, with me, seemed strange. She said, "Let's decide right now about how we will refer to him." We agreed that DMcC was it. And from then on, for all the time I worked with my father, when referring to him in writing in the professional world, it was DMcC. In writing the introductions for this book, I felt the same strangeness cropping up again. So for me and for all of you, it will be DMcC throughout.

I WORKED WITH DMcC for nearly thirty years, predominantly managing his public life and also doing all manner of other things. Mike Hill was his research assistant for almost forty years, and he, too, was someone who would always help in the "all manner of things" category. DMcC said he never could have accomplished what he did without Mike, and the McCullough family knows this to be true.

DAVID McCULLOUGH

For the past two years, Mike and I have been going through DMcC's papers. He left behind letters, calendars, multiple evolutions of original manuscripts with his handwritten editorial changes, ideas, notes, lists, diagrams, paintings, drawings, and photographs. He never worked on a computer, so everything is in its original physical form, tactile—as he liked it. Most of the material was neatly filed, in dark-gray or tan steel filing cabinets. But so, too, were some papers haphazardly put in boxes and stacked in a barn. When those cartons were opened, occasionally inside were not only his papers, but also acorns and nests and other things you might find in a New England barn. Thankfully, even in these there was little damage of consequence.

History Matters is a collection of pieces that we thought merited revisiting. Some have been published before for small audiences, but many are previously unpublished. Included are speeches, essays, tributes, interviews, and some more personal items. The book is by no means exhaustive, and there are certainly areas of his work, his life, and his personality that are not covered, including, among other things, his disciplined way of approaching everything, his love of walking and walking sticks, his insistence on things being done in particular ways, his love of lyrics and quotations, and his readily available humor. But above all, what is not sufficiently represented here is Rosalee. There is not enough of Rosalee . . . Rosalee Barnes McCullough, his wife of nearly sixty-eight years and mother of his five children. She was his true north, and it was she who truly made it all possible.

There has been a great expression from people across the country wanting more of DMcC's perspective, more of his wisdom, more of him, and especially now. In *History Matters*, we give you a little more of David McCullough.

FOREWORD

Jon Meacham

Nobody knew very much about him. In the winter and early spring of 1945, Harry Truman of Missouri—a former Jackson County judge and United States senator—was, improbably, the vice president of the United States. The third man to serve in that office under Franklin D. Roosevelt (John Nance Garner of Texas and Henry Wallace of Iowa had come and gone), Truman was a natty, no-nonsense, plain-speaking man who loved history, his family, the Democratic Party, brisk daily walks, and bourbon whiskey. Curious about the border-state politician now the proverbial heartbeat away from the presidency, the prolific American correspondent John Gunther sought Truman out for an interview. What, Gunther asked the vice president, interested him the most? The answer was characteristically pithy. "People," Truman said.

Truman's most notable biographer, David McCullough, would have given the same reply, and American life and letters are all the better for that shared passion. In McCullough's hands, history was an unfolding, contingent, and above all fascinating story of *people*—of human beings driven by fear and by hope, by ambition and by altruism, by vice and by virtue. From the Johnstown Flood and the Brooklyn Bridge and the Panama Canal; from young Theodore Roosevelt and George Washington and John Adams and Harry Truman; from Americans in Paris to the Wright brothers to white settlers on the frontier, the McCullough canon grew from a voracious curiosity about what Thomas Jefferson called "the course of human events."

Now, thanks to the deft and loving editing of Dorie McCullough Lawson and of Mike Hill, we have a kind of last testament, a final McCullough dispatch from his long and fruitful assignment as a chronicler of the American past. In the pieces collected here—many previously unpublished—we can listen once more to a man who loved art, music, drama, adventure, and courage; we can see the world as he saw it, feel it as he felt it, and love it as he loved it.

For that is an essential element of David McCullough's appeal: He wrote with a large heart, a buoyant—and sometimes boyish—enthusiasm, and a wonderfully wide-eyed wonder at the possibilities and the glories of the human story. And history *was* a story, an unfolding drama in which the men and women of a given moment could not know how everything turned out—whether the waters would recede, or whether the plane would fly, or whether the battle would be won.

The rendering of great history, then, is rooted in humility and in empathy. Which are the same things that make for great citizenship, and therein lies a truth about David McCullough's life and work. Like Horace, who said the purpose of poetry was to delight and to instruct, McCullough's books, essays, and public remarks not only delighted us but also subtly tutored us in the art of being human—of loving our neighbor as ourselves, of giving as well as taking, of lending a hand rather than clenching a fist.

With McCullough, we were given a privileged seat to watch flawed people—the temperamental Truman, the acerbic Adams, the self-absorbed TR—overcome their failings to give us a more perfect Union. Like Tennyson's "Ulysses," McCullough's subjects were a part of all that they had met, and he put great weight—decisive weight—on telling their stories with literary distinction and an appreciation that they did not dwell in some land called "History" or "the Past." Like all of us, they dwelt in a vivid, living, chaotic *present*. And McCullough's mission was to make their present real to the future—a key task, perhaps the key task, of the historian and the biographer.

And how he loved that task. "We speak a language that isn't ours," McCullough notes in these pages. "It's been handed down to us with a tradition of expression and power that is well worth a lifetime of study, and particularly for those for whom writing is a way of life. I love what I do. I love every day of it. Happiness—true happiness—is not to be found in vacations or the like. It's to be found in the love of learning and doing what you really want to get up and get to each day."

When McCullough got up to go to work, he would get to it with dispatch. Twenty years ago, on the occasion of the publication of his book *1776*, I spent a day with him for a profile about his life and work. As I wrote then, the only sound in the room on Martha's Vineyard where he wrote—a tiny book-lined shingled building, just eight feet by twelve—came from the *clack-clack-clack* of a 1940s Royal manual typewriter, bought secondhand in White Plains, New York, in 1965. The setting was snug, almost claustrophobic, but it was there, in his backyard office, that McCullough's imagination roamed the American past.

When he looked up from his Royal, he could see the restored farmhouse where he lived for fifty years with his wife, Rosalee. The house, McCullough recalled, was "part eighteenth century, part nineteenth, and part twentieth"—a good way to describe the canon of work he has created in this small office. The pages that he pulled through the carriage of the typewriter—about four a day—made McCullough a central figure in a renaissance of popular history both in print and on television. From Ken Burns's *The Civil War* to *The American Experience*, McCullough's baritone *was* the voice of the past. He loved the story of asking a question of a clerk in a grocery store about the whereabouts of something he'd been sent in to buy. On hearing McCullough speak, the man asked, "Are you David McCullough?" "Why, yes," came the reply. "Oh, I so loved your narration on the Civil War documentary." A bit puffed up by the praise, McCullough thanked him. "Yes," the clerk went on, "I'm insomniac, and when I listen to you, I go right to sleep."

The least cynical of writers, McCullough was also clear-eyed. "History is not the story of heroes entirely," he said. "It is often the story of cruelty and injustice and shortsightedness. There are monsters, there is evil, there is betrayal. That's why people should read Shakespeare and Dickens as well as history—they will find the best, the worst, the height of noble attainment and the depths of depravity." McCullough was, interestingly, a wildly popular anachronism. In a politically and culturally polarized America, he spoke in warm, unaffected tones about the classic *Ben and Me*, or about *Two Years Before the Mast*, the first book he ever bought with his own money, or about how history teachers should use Gershwin in the classroom.

Born in 1933, the son of the owner of an electrical supply company in Pittsburgh, McCullough, the third of four boys, grew up in a largely vanished world. His childhood was spent in comfort at 549 Glen Arden Drive; he attended a private high school and graduated from Yale in 1955. He worked as a writer and editor at Time Inc., then went to Washington to be part of the New Frontier, taking a job with the United States Information Agency under the CBS legend Edward R. Murrow. Standing with Rosalee outside his office, recounting the story of his job interview, he recalled being asked what he knew about Arabs. "Sir, I don't know anything at all about Arabs," McCullough replied, only to be told, "Well, you'll learn." He found himself producing a magazine—which he had never done before—directed at the Middle East. Thinking back on the time, McCullough glances at Rosalee and says, "I had to learn a lot fast, didn't I, pal?" She smiled at the memory.

McCullough asked the question with a sweet, vulnerable look, the look of a man who long depended on the woman he married in 1954. Without Rosalee, McCullough would not have become such a towering cultural figure. In the late 1960s, he was working at *American Heritage* in New York as he wrote his first book, *The Johnstown Flood*, at night and on weekends. After the account of the devastating 1889 disaster in Pennsylvania was published, the McCulloughs faced a decision: Could he quit the day job and focus full-time on books? With five children, it was not an easy call. "Rosalee's courage at that time was crucial," he recalled. "If she had been reluctant, I can't imagine I would have done it." There were hints of his future success: *Reader's Digest* had taken *The Johnstown Flood* as a condensed book. The initial payment of fifteen thousand dollars, McCullough recalled, "really changed my life." They settled on the Vineyard full-time in 1972 in a house they had bought in 1965 with a down payment of four thousand dollars. They installed a furnace in the house, built the office, and went to work. "You could live on the Vineyard for almost nothing then," he recalled, "which was good, because that's what I was making." Still, things were chancy. When McCullough would be invited to speak at colleges in those early years, his businessman father would say, "Great, maybe they'll offer you a job."

The old man needn't have worried. The boy who was transfixed by the N. C. Wyeth–illustrated editions of books like *Treasure Island* had the gift of story, and he knew how to share that gift. In 1992, with the monumental *Truman*, McCullough won the first of his two Pulitzer Prizes. The other came in 2001 for *John Adams*.

David McCullough painted with words, and the images he has left us are windows into a past that is at once remote and proximate. Remote because the stuff of his stories unfolded long ago; proximate because the forces that drove the people in those stories are perennial—love and fear, dreams and nightmares. And those forces drive us, too.

The only thing new in the world, Harry Truman once remarked, was the history we don't know. Because of David McCullough, we know a great deal, and we also know where to look to find the most important things: at ourselves. For history is not dead, but living; history is not past, but unfolding. And as McCullough taught us, nothing matters more.

"In the last analysis, I never know why I choose what I choose to write about," McCullough once recalled. "There is just a click." And when that click came, he would move out through the screen door, down the porch steps, and through the backyard and sit down in the office, where the clacking of the Royal would begin again. "History, like America," McCullough said, "is always a work in progress, an experiment, an adventure, a journey." How lucky we are that David McCullough invited us along for his.

PART ONE

WHY HISTORY?

WHY HISTORY?

In 1995, DMcC was honored with the National Book Foundation's Medal for Distinguished Contribution to American Letters. Over the course of his lifetime, he was awarded fifty-six honorary degrees and more than 125 awards, including the Pulitzer Prize twice, the National Book Award twice, and the Presidential Medal of Freedom. He met each and every recognition with delight and gratitude. When he received this overarching award for contribution to the literary world of his country, he was honored indeed. These are his remarks delivered at the awards ceremony.

History shows us how to behave. History teaches, reinforces what we believe in, what we stand for, and what we ought to be willing to stand up for. History is—or should be—the bedrock of patriotism, not the chest-pounding kind of patriotism but the real thing, love of country.

At their core, the lessons of history are largely lessons in appreciation. Everything we have, all our great institutions, hospitals, universities, libraries, cities, our laws, our music, art, poetry, our freedoms, everything exists because somebody went before us and did the hard work, provided the creative energy, provided the money, provided the belief. Do we disregard that?

Indifference to history isn't just ignorant, it's rude. It's a form of ingratitude.

I'm convinced that history encourages, as nothing else does, a sense of proportion about life, gives us a sense of the relative scale of our own brief time on earth and how valuable that is.

What history teaches, it teaches mainly by example. It inspires courage and tolerance. It encourages a sense of humor. It is an aid to navigation in perilous times. We are living now in an era of momentous change, of huge transitions in all aspects of life—nationwide and worldwide—and this creates great pressures and tensions. But history shows that times of change are the times when we are most likely to learn. This nation was founded on change. We should embrace the possibilities in these exciting times and hold to a steady course, because we have a sense of navigation, a sense of what we've been through in times past and who we are.

Think how tough our predecessors were. Think what they had been through. There's no one who hasn't an ancestor who went through some form of hell. Churchill in his great speech in the darkest hours of the Second World War, when he crossed the Atlantic, reminded us, "We haven't journeyed this far because we are made of sugar candy."

Now, history isn't just good for you in a civic way. It isn't just something you take to be a better citizen. It does do that, and that in itself would be reason enough to stress its importance. "Any nation that expects to be ignorant and free," Jefferson said, "expects what never was and never will be." And if the gap between the educated and the uneducated in America continues to grow as it has in our time, as fast as or faster than the gap between the rich and the poor, the gap between the educated and the uneducated is going to be of greater consequence and the more serious threat to our way of life. We must not, by any means, misunderstand that.

But, I think, what it really comes down to is that history is an extension of life. It both enlarges and intensifies the experience of being alive. It's like poetry and art. Or music. And it's ours, *to enjoy*. If we deny our children that enjoyment, that adventure in the larger time among the greater part of the human experience, we're cheating them out of a full life.

There's no secret to making history come alive. Barbara Tuchman said it perfectly: "Tell stories." The pull, the appeal, is irresistible, because history is about two of the greatest of all mysteries—time and human nature.

How lucky we are. How lucky we are to enjoy in our work and in our lives the possibilities, the precision and reach, the glories of the English language. How lucky we are, how very lucky we are, to live in this great country, to be Americans—Americans all.

AMERICAN VALUES

DMcC was captivated by architecture. He loved forms and light and what design expresses about a society. From the United States Capitol to Rouen Cathedral, to the Canal Zone employee housing in Panama, to the steel mills of his hometown of Pittsburgh, to the Wrights' plain house in Dayton, Ohio, to his own eight-by-twelve-foot office, he loved it all. He drew plans at the kitchen table, and he thought about architectural design all the time. He talked about architecture in some way or another every day. It was part of who he was.

With his love of architecture and commitment to history, he naturally cared deeply about historic preservation. He proudly served on the board of the National Trust for Historic Preservation, and in 1991 he delivered the following address at the National Preservation Conference in San Francisco.

Let us listen first to a voice from the past. The year is 1878.

> And then upon all sides, what a clashing of architecture! In this one valley, where the life of the town goes most busily forward, there may be seen, shown one above and behind another by the accidents of the ground, buildings in almost every style upon the globe. Egyptian and Greek temples, Venetian palaces and Gothic spires, are huddled one over another in a most admired disorder....

But Nature is a more indiscriminate patroness than we imagine, and in no way frightened of a strong effect. The birds roost as willingly among the Corinthian capitals as in the crannies of the crag; the same atmosphere and daylight clothe the eternal rock and yesterday's portico; and as the soft northern sunshine throws out everything into a glorified distinctness—or easterly mists, coming up with the blue evening, fuse all of these incongruous features into one; and the lamps begin to glitter along the street, and faint lights burn in the high windows across the valley—the feeling grows upon you that this also is a piece of nature in the most intimate sense; that this profusion of eccentricities, this dream in masonry and living rock, is not a drop scene in the theatre, but a city in the world of every-day reality.

That is Robert Louis Stevenson's evocation of Edinburgh in the heyday of the Victorian city. Note please what he is saying. The intriguing blend of the old and the new. The intriguing pull of past and future. The delight in eccentricities. The tolerance of difference. The strong point is that this is reality, not a drop scene in the theater as he says. Not television as we might say.

What is this pull of the past? Why do we care so, you and I, about history? Is it just because we are Americans and we care about our country, because we love our country as we would care about the past, the beginnings of someone we love? Or is it larger than that? And is it strange this commitment we have to understanding the past? Or conversely, why are so many out there who do not care? Is it something like having perfect pitch? Are they tone-deaf? Are they color-blind? What are we really doing with our efforts in saving buildings, writing books, making films, taking photographs, caring about who we were, where we came from?

To begin with, it belongs to an old human instinct—not wanting to be in a rut. We have no more wish to be provincial in time than we would to be provincial in space. Because fate or God or whatever it is has placed us in this particular time very briefly, we do not see why the limit of our experience as human beings should be contained within just that time. Why should we not move on to the larger stage of the past? Why should we not know how many others have gone before us? The great majority, as they used to say in Stevenson's nineteenth century.

We are also drawn, of course, because we see so many remnants, so many reminders of the past all around us. And we are drawn, I am convinced, because we are at heart storytellers. We need stories as we need food and water. Consider that for nine-tenths of all the time that anything like human beings has existed on this planet, all of their information, all they knew about who they were and how to survive, came to them through stories passed down generation after generation.

And that is a quality which has guaranteed and supported our survival as a species. It is one of our mechanisms for survival. We cannot just abandon it, just pass it by. If we do, we are going to become something less than human.

But I really think that what draws us to history, the pull of the past, is change. It is what is new, not what is old. And change is the essence of life. What we are really interested in, what we care about, is life, people, and what happened to them and why, and what changed, what was new?

Looming over Florence is the Great Dome by Filippo Brunelleschi—the cathedral of Santa Maria del Fiore. The dome itself is 375 feet high. It was built more than five hundred years ago. It was built before Columbus sailed. It is magnificent. It is the essence of Florence. It is the Renaissance. And it is a mystery. Nobody knows what the actual technique was that Brunelleschi used to create that great triumph of the Renaissance.

When it was finished, it was not Gothic. It was not Romanesque. It was something new, different from anything that had been built before. And therein is a huge part of its appeal and its importance. It speaks to us of that time as do any of the great books, the great paintings, the great statuary.

Almost exactly five hundred years later on another side of the world in a very different time by a very different people, a great bridge was built in San Francisco. The Golden Gate Bridge was begun in 1933 and finished in 1937. We should all, in my view, be grateful that we live at the time of the Golden Gate Bridge.

Both of these huge and monumental and memorable structures are symbols of affirmation, in their way. They speak of values. Consider what that bridge, that magnificent American accomplishment, represents. It is built at the entrance to the greatest sea in the world, subject to high winds, fog, storms, and a tide of seven knots. And it had to have a span, a single span, of over four thousand feet. It was to be higher above the water than any other bridge in the world.

And it does something terribly important and extremely essential for all of us never to forget. It makes that place more powerful, more meaningful. It gives both scale and a sense of humanity and time to that magnificent, natural wonder of the gateway, the entrance to the harbor.

The environmentalists say any intrusion by construction by humans will lessen the power and beauty and meaning of a particular landscape. Anything built on Storm King Mountain, it was said during the great fight over that place on the upper Hudson River, will denigrate it, lessen it. But as architectural historian and teacher Vincent Scully said, "The Greeks would have known what to build on Storm King Mountain."

The Golden Gate Bridge ought to take our breath away for many reasons. But it cannot be seen just in context of where it is. It must be seen in the context of the time that created it. As much so as Brunelleschi's dome.

The Golden Gate Bridge was built when Franklin Roosevelt was in his first term. It was built in the era of Charlie Chaplin's *Modern Times*. It was built at the time of the Berlin Olympics. Built at the time of the abdication of the King of England for "the woman I love." Built during the Great Depression. And built during a period when two of the most important events of the twentieth century took place, foretelling everything that has so changed in our world. Two events that took place not much more than one hundred miles apart.

One, in Copenhagen, where Niels Bohr and his colleagues at the

Institute for Theoretical Physics determined that if the uranium atom were split, it would release a power beyond any previous understanding or example. And just across the way at a small German fishing village, the Nazi government had instituted the first rocket experimental station under the young, brilliant physicist Wernher von Braun. So in that period when this magnificent bridge was going up, we have the beginnings of the nuclear age and the rocket century.

I grew up in Pittsburgh, Pennsylvania, surrounded by old structures. I went to get my books at the Carnegie Library. I went downtown and walked by the old H. H. Richardson jail and absolutely shuddered with fear. It looks just like Dickens. I was in a city where there are more bridges than in Paris. I grew up with bridges. I have been interested in them all of my life. I am not an engineer. I am not even a historian. I am an English major. But I am drawn to the past because I care to know what happened.

Now what of the future? What is the future for our work, your work, my work? And what will the values be that determine this future? I firmly believe, as an English major, that there ought to be no use of the expression "the foreseeable future." There is no such thing. For a historian to presume to be able to read the future is as absurd as for almost anyone to presume to read the future.

I think that what I am about to tell you concerning the future has much more to do with what I hope the future will be than any prediction of what, in fact, will happen. I hope that we will become a people who care about the past because we care about the future. I hope that we will become a people who are less self-centered, self-conscious, and selfish in terms of our own time. I have often thought and said that the digital watch is the perfect symbol of our time. It only tells you what time it is now as if there had been no time before and no time to come.

We will need people who understand that history is a spacious realm. There must be no walls. Nothing happens in isolation. Never has, never will. Our picture of the past changes almost daily. Where the spotlight for so very long has been on only a few people, a relatively few people, male, white Americans, the lights on the stage are coming up.

And all those people who have been on the stage all the time are now in the light and in focus. We see how many there are, how diverse they are, and how greatly they have made what we call "American civilization."

And that means opportunity for historians, opportunity for biographers, opportunity for people who want to go out and look at the landscape and decide what should be preserved and saved.

We have to enlist a broader spectrum of American skill and imagination. We have to be more inclusive. Edinburgh, that wonder Edinburgh described by Robert Louis Stevenson, gave forth to what was essentially an English-Scottish-Western Renaissance of its own in the eighteenth and early nineteenth century. In medicine, philosophy, people like David Hume, came the origins, the beginnings, of whole idea of an *Encyclopedia Britannica*, not to say Sir Walter Scott and Robert Louis Stevenson.

And why did it happen in that tiny, little, northern, bleak town? Why in a place smaller than New Haven, Connecticut? Well, we do not know. But one of the things we do know is that in Edinburgh in that day, everybody saw everybody. There were clubs, societies, associations. They met almost every night. Lawyers, doctors, engineers, poets—people of all professions and all persuasions saw each other, talked, worked, imagined together. No walls. No barriers. No status order. We must encourage that.

Filmmakers, photographers, must be part of what we do, must be considered the flag carriers of what we do. We do not much like television, and we do not much care for television for good reason. Most of it is terrible. But it is part of our culture, and we are in the grip of our culture as we are in the grip of our past. Television can indeed reach a very large, very appreciative audience if it is done right.

"The world is young," said Emerson. "The former great men and women call to us affectionately." There is no such thing as the dead past. The marvelous thing about the past is whenever you reach down into it, all you find is life. You could even argue that there is no such thing as the past. There was only somebody else's present. And all those people who went before us building bridges, raising great structures of all kinds, writing books, painting paintings, founding industries, all of them shared with us the puzzling and intriguing question of how is it all going to come out? They did not know any more about their future than we do about ours.

"Past things shed light on the future ones," wrote Francesco Guicciardini. If you've never read *I Ricordi* by Guicciardini, I urge you to do so. It was written in the sixteenth century in Florence in the shadow of the Brunelleschi dome. "Past things shed light on the future ones. The world was always of a kind. What is and will be, was at some other time. The same things come back but under different names and different colors. Not everybody recognizes them, but only who is wise and considers them diligently."

We will, I hope, see a new generation of Americans who are more humane, more tolerant, more eclectic. I hope very much that we will devise an educational system that does far more than is being done at the present to reward students in the school system from grade one on for two qualities that are largely ignored in the present system.

The first is imagination, originality, spontaneity—call it what you want. The second is a willingness to take risks. I have run a test in some of the courses I have taught where I have asked an audience, or a large lecture class, to take out a piece of paper and write down all the things you can think to do with a brick. It is very interesting because there is no correlation between those who have had traditionally high grades in their previous scholastic careers and those who come up with imaginative or ingenious thoughts on what to do with a brick.

Risk-taking is another very rare quality among students and must be encouraged. They are extremely skilled at reading a teacher's mind. They are extremely capable of giving you what they think you want, which is not taking risks. Therefore, tests must be devised, processes of experimentation must be devised, whereby the student is not competing against anybody else but himself or herself.

All great civilizations have had at least two things in common: confidence and a sense of continuity. And we gain both from our sense of the past. We are confident because we know who we are. We know what we have done. We know we have been there before.

And because we know what has been done in the past, we know what the standards are. We know what we must live up to. And if we have a sense of the past, then we also have a sense that what we do will be looked at in the future as the standard by which to measure one's performance. How we wish to be measured in the future is a concept that can only come to those who have some sense of measuring themselves against the past. And continuity, of course, is the essence of writing history and caring about the future.

I do not think human nature is going to change in the future at all. I do think that we are living in one of the most revolutionary of all times. What happened in Eastern Europe and the Soviet Union was a tumultuous change of a kind that we will not even begin to understand or comprehend for many more years. But be assured it is immensely important. It is an earthquake in time. A Krakatoa in history. And that is exciting. That is change. That is what we are interested in. What's new, we say, we Americans. What is new?

In 1964, I went with my young family to the New York World's Fair. And like millions of others, we stood in line to get into the General Motors exhibit. And eventually we came to the point where it was our turn. Several small children, a husband, and a wife. If you went to the General Motors exhibit or if you've read about it, you may remember that it was a series of automobiles on a conveyor belt. You got into the car, and you rode through the future in a brand-new, shiny General Motors car, naturally.

And the future that was displayed, the future that was to be now, right now, our time, was one of exquisitely shining, glassy, spotless buildings set in a landscape in which there was virtually nothing from the past. And the centerpiece were magnificent highways, eight, ten, fifteen lanes wide on which the automobiles traveled without the necessity to drive the car. They were on conveyor belts or some sort of beam that was going to guide them spaced safely at reasonable distances.

There was a large machine that was chewing up the jungle and creating buildings as it went along. This was the world of the future. The world of tomorrow. Well, we climbed into the car, a white Impala with red seats. And I asked our little boy Billy, who was five years old, if he would like to drive. He got behind the steering wheel, and on we went through the world of tomorrow for roughly a half an hour, or whatever it took. And after it was over and we came out blinking into the sunshine, we were all saying, "Boy, wasn't that something?"

I turned to little Bill, and I said, "Well, what did you think, Bill?" He said, "I don't know. I was too busy driving." He understood the future better than the people at General Motors. The world of the future as portrayed by General Motors had no bearing on our time. But Billy McCullough was saying we must have a sense of responsibility. He felt very responsible. The whole family was dependent on his ability to guide that automobile.

Saint-Exupéry's *Wind, Sand and Stars* is one of the greatest books that deal with the problem in nature. He said that responsibility is the essence of morality. If we do not care about our past, if we do not write history and biography, take photographs, make films, save buildings, save whole towns, and save the works, too, of the industry and science of our rich, diverse, and protean culture, then we are being irresponsible in the extreme.

I am a short-range pessimist and a long-range optimist. I sincerely believe that we may be on the way to a very different and far better time. Let us hope so. Let us pray so.

TAKE LUCK TO HEART

DMcC often said that history is not just politics and the military; it is, among other things, industry, arts, science, business, medicine, failure, money, and love. He was also interested in another element of history: luck. What role did luck play in people's lives? He liked to quote Winston Churchill, who when praised for his courage famously said that his nation had the lion's heart and he "had the luck to be called upon to give the roar."

The subject of luck and history figure large in DMcC's 2018 commencement address at Providence College.

Think how lucky we are, every one of us, and it is luck that I want to talk about today. The continuing desire for good luck in our lives and the lives of those we love is part of human nature. We are all desirous of it. We are all known to knock on wood or cross our fingers when the need arises. We blow into cupped hands before a throw of the dice, keep our eyes out for four-leaf clover; we thank our lucky stars; we nail a horseshoe over the door. Brilliant Danish physicist Niels Bohr, who had a horseshoe over his door, was asked once by a skeptical colleague whether he believed in such nonsense. "Oh no," Bohr said. "But I'm told that it works even if you don't believe it." We take luck to heart, and we should, because luck, good luck and bad luck, play an important, an immensely important, part in life, and so it does in history. Primarily because history is human.

Scanning over the catalog of courses offered by Providence College, I see no mention of the word *luck*, nor among the more than five hundred courses in history offered at one of our premier universities, does the word appear. I've long thought it would make a fascinating course. Certainly, there would be no shortage of material with which to work. Luck in its various forms has been recognized as a fact of life by many of history's prominent figures. Franklin Roosevelt was known to have carried a rabbit's foot with him during the 1932 election.

If there ever was a momentous stroke of luck favoring the American cause, it was what happened at Brooklyn in the final days of August 1776. The American Army under the command of George Washington had been outsmarted and outfought by the British in the Battle of Brooklyn, the first great battle of the Revolutionary War, and for the Americans, it was a crushing defeat. On the morning of August 28, the situation was critical. Washington and the army, some nine thousand troops, were trapped on Brooklyn Heights in an area about three miles around, their backs to the East River, which could serve as an escape route to Manhattan, only if the wind cooperated. Until then, a northeast wind had been blowing with sufficient force to keep the British from bringing warships up into the East River and shut off any hope of escape. American riflemen on the outermost defenses were ordered to keep up steady fire at the enemy, and the British fired back on into the afternoon, when the clouds opened and a cold, drenching rain, the start of a nor'easter storm, had brought still more misery to the defeated army.

The storm continued through the night and into the following morning. At four o'clock that afternoon, Washington called a meeting with his generals at a mansion on the brow of the Heights, overlooking the river. A decision whether to retreat had to be made on the grounds that ammunition had been spoiled by the heavy rains, the miseries of the exhausted troops, the enemy's strength, and the looming threat of the British fleet suddenly in command of the river.

The decision was unanimous. So, the night of August 29, 1776, escape began. As one officer would later write, putting himself in Washington's place, "To move so large a body of troops, with all their necessary appendages, across a river a full mile wide, with a rapid current, in the face of a victorious, well-disciplined army, nearly three times as numerous as his own men, and a fleet capable of stopping the navigation so that not one boat could have passed over, seemed to present the most formidable obstacles."

The northeast wind was blowing still as the first of the troops began moving in silence through the dark of night down to the ferry landing. At about eleven o'clock, as if by design, the northeast wind died down. Then the wind shifted to the southwest, and the small armada of boats, manned by Massachusetts sailors and fishermen, started over the river from New York. They crossed back and forth all through the night, the boats so loaded with troops and supplies, horses and cannon, that the water was often only inches below the gunnels. All in the pitch-dark with no running lights. The men coming to the ferry landing moved through the night like specters.

But the exodus was not moving fast enough. Though nearly morning, a large part of the army still waited to embark, and without the curtain of night to conceal them, escape was doomed. Incredibly, yet again, luck. The hand of God, it would also be called, intervened on a grand scale. Just at daybreak a heavy fog settled in over the whole of Brooklyn, concealing everything no less than had the night. It was a fog so thick that one could scarcely discern a man six yards distant. Even with the sun up, the fog remained as dense as ever, while over on the New York side of the river, there was no fog at all.

At about seven o'clock in the morning, the last of the escaping army had safely landed in New York, and in less than an hour, the fog disappeared, and the enemy could be seen gathered on the opposite shore. In a single night, nine thousand troops had miraculously escaped across the river, not a life was lost. Had the northeast winds stopped earlier and the British brought their warships up the river, had there been no thick fog the morning after, it is likely the war would have been over right then and there, and history would have been greatly changed there and then.

It is often said we can make good luck happen, and in the lives of many of those I have written about in my books, this is clear. Take the astonishing example of Wilbur Wright. In his youth, he had excelled at just about everything; he had been a star athlete and an outstanding student. In his last year of high school in Dayton, Ohio, he scored in the nineties in algebra, botany, chemistry, English composition, geology, geometry, and Latin. That he was bound for college seemed certain, but all such plans ended when in a pickup hockey game on a frozen neighborhood lake he was smashed in the face with a hockey stick, knocking out most of his upper front teeth. For weeks, he suffered excruciating pain in his face and jaw, then had to be fitted with false teeth. Spells of depression followed and grew longer. He withdrew from society and remained a self-imposed recluse for nearly three years.

For his family, it was the most worrisome time they had known. The Wrights lived in a small house with no running water, no indoor plumbing, no electricity, no central heat, no telephone, but it was a house full of books. Great literature, history, biography, works on ornithology and theology, all as provided by their father, an itinerant preacher who believed in a liberal arts education at home. It was there and then in his isolation that Wilbur set to reading as never before. Books of all kinds, and articles, including one on the German glider enthusiast Otto Lilienthal, which led to numerous books on birds. One of these stressed that the way of an eagle in the air must remain a mystery until the structure and use of wings were understood. Like the inspiring lectures of a great professor, the book opened his eyes and started him thinking in ways he never had. Thus, the worst thing that had ever happened to him was transformed, by him, into the best thing in that it gave him a mission, a sense of purpose in life that sustained his efforts his entire life. Working with his brother Orville, they changed the world.

I myself have benefited immensely, immeasurably, from much good luck over the years. It was the discovery of a collection of photographs, quite by chance, in the Library of Congress, that led to my book on the

HISTORY MATTERS

Johnstown Flood. It was the chance remarks of two friends at lunch one day that led to my telling the story of the building of the Brooklyn Bridge. Lucky finds and collections of great libraries and archival collections have happened for me again and again.

The greatest of all strokes of luck in my life was the arrival on the scene of a princess from afar, Rosalee Ingram Barnes, my wife of sixty-three years, my editor in chief, and the star I steer by.

How lucky we all are to live in this great country, where freedom of speech, the rule of law, and representative government remain the way of life. Where the love of learning holds strong. Where there are public libraries free to the people in virtually every city and town. No less than seventeen hundred public libraries.

The lessons of history are beyond counting. One is that almost nothing of consequence is ever accomplished alone. It is a joint effort. Nor is there any such thing as a self-made man or woman. We are all the result of the many who have helped along the way, who have taught and encouraged us, seen to our needs, enlarged our horizons, or are there for us in times of need. Parents especially, and teachers. Bless our teachers. We have all benefited from the best of them. Those enthusiastic, inspiring teachers who change your life. We have serious problems to face as a people, make no mistake, and high among them is our public school system, which in parts of the country are a disgrace. But we will solve that problem, and others; that's been our way, that's our history.

I close now with a few thoughts for you, the class of 2018.

Be generous. Give of yourselves. Count kindness as all-important in life. Take interest in those around you. Try to keep in mind that everyone you encounter along the way, no matter their background or station in life, knows something you don't. Get in the habit of asking people about themselves, their lives, their interests, and listen to them. It's amazing what you can learn by listening.

Remember that speaking the truth, loyalty, decency, courage, and character all count. All matter greatly still, indeed, count more now than ever. We as a nation are experiencing serious bumps in the road.

Don't get discouraged, don't give up. We've known worse times and come through, and we will now if we never forget who we are and what we stand for. The world needs you, you the class of 2018, there's work to be done. Let's never lapse into being spectators only. If you're going to ring the bell, give that rope one hell of a pull.

THE GOOD WORK
OF AMERICA

A previously unpublished essay written in 1990 about the hard, essential work of being an American citizen.

If we want to make it a better country, if we're serious, we would do well to begin with a few simple lessons from the past.

The first is that nothing of lasting value or importance in our way of life, none of our proudest attainments, has ever come without effort. America is an effort. We are a nation born of risk and adversity—of fearful seas to cross just to get here in the first place, of land to clear, floods, epidemic disease, of slave chains and city slums and terrible winters on the high plains.

Everything we have took work: our institutions, our wealth, our freedoms. "Look at all the farms," a child says to her grandmother in the seats behind me on a summer flight into Minneapolis. "Yes," she replies. "And what work it took!"

Work got us where we are. Easy does it has never done it for us and never will. We are the beneficiaries of men and women who toiled ten, twelve hours a day on farms, on railroads, in mines, in mills, at kitchen sinks and drafting tables. We like to work; we judge one another by how well we work, because at heart we are an extremely industrious, creative people. And it is from our accomplishments, from our best work, that we've found our greatest satisfaction and sense of worth as a people—not from ease or comfort or from owning things, though we do go through spells when we forget that. The rolling-up of sleeves to tackle the new and difficult in America is not just poster art; it's been our story, in fact.

So we should take heart—"Spit on our hands and take a fresh holt," as our plainspoken forebears might have said. Nor should we expect our politicians to solve our problems for us. Which is another lesson from the past.

History shows that Congress acts when the country wants action. Leadership takes charge in Washington when it is clear the country will accept nothing less. The sweeping reforms enacted at the start of the twentieth century—limits on child labor, women's suffrage, protection of our natural resources—all came about because the country demanded such change. And the same was true during the next great upswelling of progressive action in Congress, in the early 1930s, when Social Security, rural electrification, and the minimum wage were established.

If the politicians of our time fail to meet the challenges of our time, we have only ourselves to blame. If we don't vote, if we are unwilling to pay taxes, or even to take part in the census, then what good are we as citizens? What will history say of us?

As the greatest of our politicians said in his famous first inaugural address in the dark hour before the storm of the Civil War, "This country, with its institutions, belongs to the people who inhabit it."

Another lesson from our past, most surely, is that we are better at some things than others, and we're better off doing what we do best. What we've excelled at for a very long time is making things, building, solving problems. And educating our children.

Our creative vitality has been an example for the world. We make movies, music, medicines, trucks, toys, airplanes, paint, plate glass, and computers as does no one; we publish books, design and manufacture clothes, as does no one. Our creative energy and output, it should also be noted, has seldom had much to do with our politics, the so-called climate in Washington. It was in the 1920s, for example, the time of the Teapot Dome scandal, the era when the president of the United States, Calvin Coolidge, spent a good part of every afternoon asleep; when Gershwin composed *An American in Paris*; when Faulkner, Hemingway, and Fitzgerald burst upon the scene; when Lindbergh built his plane and flew the Atlantic; and when Michelson measured the speed of light.

We are the people who built the Panama Canal and the Golden Gate Bridge, the Mount Wilson Observatory, the Library of Congress, Lincoln Center. We invented jazz and the general hospital. We grew strong making steel and automobiles. Our productive power turned the tide of world history in this century, in the Second World War. We are the people who devised *Voyager II*, the unmanned spacecraft that succeeded in photographing the planet Uranus, in the dark, while traveling at a speed of forty thousand miles an hour.

Our public schools and great universities have long been considered the best in the world. And if our past can teach us anything, it is that education—education second to none and open to all—has been our salvation, our making. That, too, has been part of the work of America, the good work of America.

We are what we do. The test will be in what we value, what we want.

"THE ART OF BIOGRAPHY"

The Paris Review Interview

In his long, productive, public career, DMcC was interviewed countless times, on television, onstage, for the radio, in person, and for print. It was simply part of the work of being an author. But to be interviewed by The Paris Review was different. He was particularly proud of this one.

Interviewer: Would you tell us about the motto tacked over your desk?

McCullough: It says, "Look at your fish." It's the test that Louis Agassiz, the nineteenth-century Harvard naturalist, gave every new student. He would take an odorous old fish out of a jar, set it in a tin pan in front of the student and say, "Look at your fish." Then Agassiz would leave. When he came back, he would ask the student what he'd seen. "Not very much," they would most often say, and Agassiz would say it again: "Look at your fish." This could go on for days. The student would be encouraged to draw the fish but could use no tools for the examination, just hands and eyes. Samuel Scudder, who later became a famous entomologist and expert on grasshoppers, left us the best account of the "ordeal with the fish." After several days, he still could not see whatever it was Agassiz wanted him to see. But, he said, "I see how little I saw before." Then Scudder had a brainstorm, and he announced it to Agassiz the next morning: "Paired organs, the same on both sides." "Of course! Of course!" Agassiz said, very pleased. So Scudder naturally asked what he should do next, and Agassiz said, "Look at your fish."

I love that story and have used it often when teaching classes on writing, because seeing is so important in this work. Insight comes, more often than not, from looking at what's been on the table all along, in front of everybody, rather than from discovering something new. Seeing is as much the job of an historian as it is of a poet or a painter, it seems to me. That's Dickens' great admonition to all writers, "Make me see."

Interviewer: Have you had Scudder moments?

McCullough: Oh, yes. I suppose the most vivid one—when I actually felt something like a charge of electricity run up my spine—was while working on the puzzle of young Theodore Roosevelt's asthma. Hoping to pin down the cause of his attacks, I had been talking to a physician who raised such questions as whether there was a dog or a cat in the house or the attacks occurred during the pollen season. Then a specialist in psychosomatic aspects of the illness suggested a different approach. "Did the attacks come before or after some big event? Or before the boy's birthday, or the night before a trip, or just before or after Christmas?" Using his diary entries, I made a calendar of what he was doing every day. In pencil I wrote where he was, who was with him, what was going on, and in red ink I put squares around the days of the asthma attacks. But, a little like Scudder and the fish, I couldn't see a pattern. Then first thing one morning, without really thinking about it, I looked at the calendar lying on my desk, and I saw what I'd been missing. The red boxes were all in a row—the attacks were all happening on Sunday. I thought, What happens on Sunday? Then it began to make sense. If he had an attack, he didn't have to go to church, which he hated, and his father would take him to the country. He loved the country, and when it was just he and his father alone—that was pure heaven. This doesn't mean the attacks were planned. The closest analogy to an asthma attack might be a case of the hiccoughs: you don't decide to have them, and yet, just as the hiccoughs can be ended by something traumatic, some kinds of asthmatic attacks are triggered by anxiety. Roosevelt paid an awful price for those trips because attacks such as he had were horrible. There may well have been other things contributing to the attacks, but the Sunday pattern was too pronounced to be coincidental.

There's another scene in *Mornings on Horseback* that I felt was crucial to understanding Roosevelt's character, which might not be considered important by conventional standards. The family was taking a trip up the Nile, and young Theodore, who was an amateur taxidermist, shot and stuffed a number of birds. So I went out and found out how taxidermy is done. It takes patience and dexterity, and it's smelly and grubby—a kind of work that would be very difficult for a child. And if you do it on a boat with your whole family present, you upstage them all. There's a paragraph or two in the book about the process of stuffing a bird, because I thought that would show a lot about the boy. I didn't want to say, "He was a bright boy who did things other boys couldn't." I wanted the reader to know it.

Novelists talk about their characters starting to do things they didn't expect them to. Well, I imagine every writer of biography or history, as well as fiction, has the experience of suddenly seeing a few pieces of the puzzle fit together. The chances of finding a new piece are fairly remote—though I've never written a book where I didn't find *something* new—but it's more likely you see something that's been around a long time that others haven't seen. Sometimes it derives from your own nature, your own interests. More often, it's just that nobody bothered to look closely enough.

Interviewer: What led you to become a writer?

McCullough: Thornton Wilder was a fellow at my college at Yale. Here was a world-celebrated writer for us to talk to, to have lunch with—imagine!—and he was easy to talk to, delightful. Later, while working in New York, I read the interview with him in *The Paris Review*. I can't tell you what a difference it made for me. When asked why he wrote books and plays, he said, "I think I write in order to discover on my shelf a new book which I would enjoy reading or to see a new play that would engross me." If it didn't exist, he wrote it so he could read it or see it.

Interviewer: What were you doing in New York?

McCullough: After graduation I got a job at Time-Life, as a trainee at *Sports Illustrated*, a new magazine. I worked there and on others of the Time-Life magazines for five years, and for a number of different editors. One of them had a big rubber stamp and a red ink pad. The stamp had a four-letter word on it and, if he didn't like what you'd written, he'd stamp it and send it back. The word was *dull*. When you'd had that done to you a couple of times, you began to get the point.

HISTORY MATTERS

Earlier, as a graduation present, I'd been given *A Stillness at Appomattox* by Bruce Catton. And though I didn't know it at the time, that book really changed the course of my life. I thought it was just marvelous and wondered, How do you do that? I read more of Catton, and other books about the Civil War. Margaret Leech's *Reveille in Washington* stands out in memory. I was finding my way, I suppose.

Interviewer: When did you decide, to use Thornton Wilder's words, to "write the book you wanted to read"?

McCullough: It was when I came across a set of old photographs of the Johnstown flood. When we were little kids, we used to make a lake of gravy in our mashed potatoes; then we'd take a fork, break the potatoes, and say, "The Johnstown flood!"—with no idea why in the world we did it. That was about all I knew about it until I saw the photographs of the flood, quite by chance at the Library of Congress. I became extremely curious to know what had happened and why. I went to the library and found a book, and it was only so-so. The author had some of the geography of western Pennsylvania wrong, I could see, and he didn't answer certain questions I felt he should have. I took out another book, a pot boiler written at the time of the disaster, and it was even less satisfactory. So I decided to try to write the book I wanted to read. I wasn't at all sure how to go about it. One evening, in New York, at a gathering of writers and historians interested in the West, my boss, Alvin Josephy, pointed to a white-haired man across the room. He said, "That's Harry Drago. Harry Sinclair Drago. He's written over a hundred books." I waited for my chance and walked over. "Mr. Drago," I said, "Alvin Josephy says that you've written over a hundred books." "Yes," he said, "that's right." "How do you do that?" I asked.

And he said, "Four pages a day." "Every day?" "Every day." It was the best advice an aspiring writer could be given.

I wrote *The Johnstown Flood* at night after work. I would come home, we'd have dinner, put the kids to bed, and then about nine I would go to a little room upstairs, close the door and start working. I tried to write not four but two pages every night. Our oldest daughter remembers going to sleep to the sound of the typewriter.

Interviewer: What kind of research did you do for that book?

McCullough: Well, one of the great resources I came across was testimony taken by the Pennsylvania Railroad from their employees after the flood. It was done in anticipation of lawsuits. They brought people in and sat them down and said, "Tell us what you saw and what you did." Thus we've been left with many reports of the disaster from a cross section of the population, all in their own words.

Interviewer: Did that wealth of vernacular reports determine the narrative form in which you've continued to write history? Would your first book have otherwise been told in that style?

McCullough: I never had any intention of writing except in the narrative form. I believe in the strong narrative. In E. M. Forster's *Aspects of the Novel*, he talks about the difference between a sequence of events and a story. He says, If I tell you that the king died and then the queen died, that's a sequence of events. If I tell you that the king died and then the queen died of grief, that's a story—you *feel* that. The basic information about the Johnstown flood can be looked up in an encyclopedia, an almanac, or reports. But you're not going to feel anything by reading those. Not only do I want the reader to get inside the experience of the events and feel what it was like—*I* want to get inside the events and feel what it was like. People often ask me if I'm "working on a book," and I say yes, because that's what they asked, but in fact they've got the wrong preposition. I'm *in* the book, *in* the subject, *in* the time and the place. Whenever I go away for a couple of days, I have to work to put myself back in it, to get back under that spell.

Interviewer: Did you have other subjects in mind as you were working on *The Johnstown Flood*?

McCullough: Not long after that book was published, two different editors asked if I'd like to do the Chicago fire or the San Francisco earthquake. I felt I was being typecast when I had just barely started—I was going to be Bad-News McCullough. I said no. What had interested me most about the story of the flood were the social and political aspects of it. The book was really about human shortsightedness, the message being that it's extremely risky, even perilous, to assume that because people hold positions of responsibility they are therefore behaving responsibly.

After I had finished the book, I felt the need for a symbol of affirmation, for something that was done right. One day I was having lunch in a German restaurant on the Lower East Side with an architect-engineer and a science writer. They started talking about what the builders of the Brooklyn Bridge *didn't know* when they started it. The more they talked, the more I realized I had found my subject. I had lived in Brooklyn Heights and walked over the bridge many times; the Roeblings came from my part of Pennsylvania, and I knew something about them because they plotted the course of the Pennsylvania Railroad through Johnstown. I left the restaurant and went straight to the Forty-Second Street Library and climbed those marble stairs to the third floor as if I had a jet engine on my back. There were over a hundred cards on the Brooklyn Bridge, but none described a book of the kind I had already begun blocking out in my mind. I went to Peter Schwed, my editor at Simon & Schuster, and said, "I've got my next book." He said he had an idea, too: the Panama Canal. I told him mine, and we agreed that I'd go ahead with the bridge first, then the canal. A lot of work was cut out that day.

I heard about a collection of Roebling material at Rensselaer Polytechnic Institute at Troy, New York, where Washington Roebling had gone. One day in the fall of 1968, my wife, Rosalee, and I drove up there. At the library, a gloomy old Gothic building that had once been a church, the woman at the desk told us the Roebling material was up in the attic, in a storage closet. She handed me the key. It was really a small windowless room with shelves on all sides, packed solid with boxes and bundles of letters, old books, scrapbooks, the door knocker of the Roebling house in Brooklyn, a statue of the old man, John A. Roebling. I looked at it and thought, My God, what a treasure. Rosalee looked at it and thought, My God—there goes who knows how many years! None of it had been cataloged or sorted. I was told I could have the key and come and go as need be. It was interesting. I knew nothing of engineering or bridges. Like a lot of people, I had been told as a youngster, "You're good at English and history; best stay away from science and math." I had no mathematics beyond algebra, no science courses except for geology. The Roebling papers were a great lesson because I found not only that I could handle technical material, but that it was extremely interesting.

Of course, I had help from experts and engineers, but my thought was, If I can make this clear and interesting to myself, then maybe it will be interesting to others. I remember one night at a party here on the Vineyard, we were introduced to a socially prominent woman from Washington. When she heard what I was working on, she said in a big, whiskey voice, "Who in the world would ever want to read a book about the Brooklyn Bridge?" In a way she did me a great favor. I was determined to prove her wrong.

Interviewer: What makes an historical subject compelling, then? Why do you think she didn't expect the story to be interesting?

McCullough: Well, some subjects appear on the surface to be more compelling than others. I think one of the reasons that historians write about war so much is that it's not very hard to hold the reader's interest. I have no particular desire to write about war. As a writer, I'm interested in the creative drive, the continuity of a civilization, the connection between one generation and the next. Maybe that's why fathers and sons play such a large part in my books. How does one generation break away from the preceding one, and what does it gain or lose by doing so?

Interviewer: *The Path Between the Seas*, about the Panama Canal, was your first best seller.

McCullough: That project required an enormous amount of research. I expected it to take three years, and I was wrong. *The Path Between the Seas* wound up taking twice that. About halfway through, our money ran out, the advance was gone. We were holding our breath, wondering how to pay the bills, the tuitions, how to keep going. But the more I looked, the more I found, and the longer the work went on. Then I saw that the book was too long. I had become very involved in the French side of the Panama Canal story, which is fascinating, but the book was out of balance. I went back and cut about a hundred pages. That was painful. You really can't just cut—you have to rewrite.

Interviewer: How do you decide what to include, what to omit, what belongs to history, and what's extraneous?

McCullough: Thornton Wilder talked, in that *Paris Review* interview, about the difficulty of re-creating the past: "It lies in the effort to employ the past tense in such a way that it does not rob those events of their character of having occurred in freedom." That's the difficulty exactly: How do you write about something that happened long ago in a way so that it has the openness, the feeling of events happening in freedom? How to write solid history and, at the same time, give life to the past and see the world as it was to those vanished people, with an understanding of what they didn't know. The problem with so much of history as it's taught and written is that it's so often presented as if it were all on a track—this followed that. In truth, nothing ever had to happen the way it happened. Nothing was preordained. There was always a degree of tension, of risk, and the question of what was going to happen next. The Brooklyn Bridge was built. You know that, it's standing there today, but they didn't know that at the start. No one knew Harry Truman would become president or that the Panama Canal would be completed.

I feel I am working in the tradition of historians, biographers like Bruce Catton, Barbara Tuchman, Paul Horgan, who work in the narrative form. I love to tell a story. History, I really believe, is best understood as an unfolding story. I think there's more intellectual honesty in seeing it that way, from *within* what happened. The moment has gone, the characters are dead, but you can bring them back, re-create their ever-changing lives in such a way that the story does not sound monotonous, with an unrelieved tempo. Life does not come at us that way—why should history? Some, of course, prefer history as seen from the mountaintop, and write it that way, which is fine. It's just not the way I wish to do it.

Interviewer: Do you still read much fiction?

McCullough: Oh, all the time. Reading fiction is also a part of my historical research. Just now, to immerse myself in the world of the book I'm working on, about John and Abigail Adams and their circle, I'm reading little else, in the way of fiction, but eighteenth-century novels—Defoe, Richardson, Fielding, Tobias Smollett, Sterne.

Interviewer: What's the process of writing like for you?

McCullough: I work in the small building out back, and it's just right for me. There's no running water and no telephone. No distractions. Because it has windows on all four sides, and a high ceiling, there's no feeling of being boxed in. It's off limits to everyone but grandchildren. They come out anytime they wish—the smaller the better. I work all day and just about every day. I go out about 8:30 in the morning, like I'm going to the train, come back in for lunch, look at the mail, then I go back again for the afternoon. We built it when I was writing *The Great Bridge*. Before that I rented a little studio from a neighbor who had built several of them, each on wooden skids. You could pick out a spot on his farm, and he'd hook a studio to his tractor and drag it there for you.

Interviewer: You use a typewriter.

McCullough: I write on an old Royal typewriter, a beauty! I bought it secondhand in 1965, before I started *The Johnstown Flood*, and I've written all my books on it. It was made about 1941, and it works perfectly. I have it cleaned and oiled about once every book, and the roller has to be replaced now and then. Otherwise it's the same machine. Imagine—it's more than fifty years old, and it still does just what it was built to do! There's not a thing wrong with it.

I love putting paper in. I love the way the keys come up and actually print the letters. I love it when I swing that carriage and the bell rings like an old trolley car. I love the feeling of making something with my hands. People say, "But with a computer you could go so much faster." But I don't want to go faster. If anything, I should go slower. I don't think all that fast. They say, "But you could change things so readily." I can change things very readily as it is. I take a pen and draw a circle around what I want to move up or down or wherever, and then I retype it. Then they say, "But you wouldn't have to retype it." But when I'm retyping I'm also rewriting. And I'm listening, hearing what I've written. Writing should be done for the ear. Rosalee reads aloud wonderfully, and it's a tremendous help to me to hear her speak what I've written. Or sometimes I read it to her. It's so important. You hear things that are wrong, that call for editing.

HISTORY MATTERS

Interviewer: Do you make corrections while she's reading?

McCullough: Yes, I make a little mark, or she does. Once when she was reading one of the last chapters of *Mornings on Horseback*, she stopped and said, "There's something wrong with that sentence." I said, "Read it again." She read it again, "There's something wrong there." I said, "Give it to me, you're not reading it right," and I read it out loud and said, "See?"

Well, a year or so later, when the book was published, Gore Vidal reviewed it in *The New York Review of Books*. It was a favorable review, and I was very pleased, except that, out of the whole book, he singled out one sentence as an example that my writing wasn't always the best. And it was that sentence! The only one he quoted!

Interviewer: What was wrong with it?

McCullough: Nothing!

Interviewer: What was the sentence?

McCullough: You would have to ask. "The horse he rode so hard day after day that he all but ruined it."

Interviewer: Can you talk about the mental process involved when you're at work in your study?

McCullough: There's no question that the sheer effort of writing, of getting it down on paper, makes the brain perform as it rarely does otherwise. I don't understand people who sit and think what they're going to write and then just write it out. My head doesn't work that way. I've got to mess around with it on paper. I've got to make sketches, think it out on paper. Sometimes I think I'm not a writer, I'm a *re*writer. When a page isn't working, I crumple it into a ball and throw it in the wastebasket. Always have. Our son Geoffrey when he was a little boy would come out where I work and look in my wastebasket to see how many "wrong pages" I had written that day. If the basket was full, it had been a good day. I'd worked things through.

Interviewer: When do you and Rosalee begin reading aloud to each other?

McCullough: Usually after I've finished a chapter, especially in the early stages of a book. It's only when you begin to write that you begin to see what you don't know and need to find out. In the early stages I'm sort of trying my legs. I have to feel each chapter is pretty close to being right before I can go on. Each page has to be close to right before I can do the next. And, of course, all the time you're asking yourself, Am I getting it right? Is this clear? Am I being fair? Is this really the way it was? The way it really happened? Am I putting too much faith in this person's analysis or that person's recollection? Am I being overly influenced by latter-day sources? I have to put everything into focus so that my point, some essential aspect of Louis Agassiz's fish becomes clear.

Interviewer: Is it possible to do too much research?

McCullough: I love the research. And it certainly can become seductive. The tendency is to wander off on tangents—digging into the life of some minor character beyond what's necessary. In the case of *The Great Bridge*, I actually did some additional research after the book was published. I spent an evening with the Boston Psychoanalytic Society to discuss the character of Washington Roebling with them. I told them a few new things I had learned about his illness, and they helped me make sense of them. Washington Roebling took over as chief engineer after his father, John, the designer of the bridge, died. He developed a case of caisson disease, or "the bends," an excruciatingly painful affliction, and went into seclusion in his house in Brooklyn Heights. He directed the whole project from his window. I realized that some of his symptoms had nothing to do with the bends, and they seemed to be psychosomatic. From what I learned from the psychoanalysts, I came to the conclusion that Roebling was almost certainly addicted to opiates. His pain was so severe that he was given a lot of drugs: morphine and, later, laudanum. In addition, he was encumbered by his father's reputation. If the bridge succeeded, it would be his father's success; if it failed, it would be his disgrace. He really had good reason to detest his father. It can't be coincidental that as soon as the bridge was finished, he came out of the house and resumed a normal life. Now, I'm not a psychobiographer—I don't generally venture into that kind of speculation—but these two factors, the addiction and the hatred for his father, tell a great deal about Roebling's character.

Interviewer: Were you tempted to add a discussion of that to subsequent editions of *The Great Bridge*?

McCullough: I thought about writing a new foreword to the twenty-fifth anniversary printing, but there are a lot of things I'd like to do that I don't have time for. Still, it was fascinating. And perhaps it contributed to my thinking about the psychosomatic aspects of Theodore Roosevelt's asthma. I've found medical research as absorbing as anything I've ever done. It's another way of understanding people. If you think about medical diagnosis, it's much the same as what a writer has to do: diagnose his characters. For my current book, I want to find out more about smallpox, which was a defining circumstance of life in that era. That's the great thing about a writer's life: nothing is useless, everything bears on the work.

Interviewer: You've done "field research," too, such as growing a beard when you were working on *The Great Bridge*. Did that help?

McCullough: It all helps. And anything that helps is welcome. I couldn't possibly have written about people trying to dig the Panama Canal without going down there and feeling the humidity, the rain, and the heat. For *Truman*, I had to see the places where he was in World War I, and to make the run he made through the Capitol on the night that Roosevelt died. Sam Rayburn had a little hideaway on the House side of the Capitol, which is where Truman, who was presiding over the Senate, had gone that evening. He got a call there, summoning him to the White House. He didn't know why. Nobody told him that Roosevelt was dead. In his diary or one of his letters, I forget which, he writes that after excusing himself he ran to his office to get his hat—which is a nice period touch—before going to his car to drive over to the White House. Well, that run, it seemed to me, was one of the key moments in the whole story. Why was he running? Was he running toward something or away from something? Did he somehow guess that he was running to the presidency? It's a great moment. I wanted to see how long it would have taken him to make that run, to figure out which route he took, because he could have gone several ways, to see what would have been flashing by in his peripheral vision. To do it, I had to make arrangements with the Senate historian, a wonderful fellow named Dick Baker, because you can't just start running through the Capitol. It was a long run. Among other things, I realized that Truman must have been in very good shape. At the end of the run he had to go charging up a long flight of stairs.

Interviewer: How do you know when it's time to stop?

McCullough: It's a little like knowing when you've eaten enough. I know exactly when it's happening, just as I do when I get an idea for a book. It just happens. It's not rational, not even explainable. I sometimes get the feeling that the subject picks me, as if I was meant to write each book at a certain time in my life.

Interviewer: Do you miss your characters when it's over?

McCullough: Oh, you bet. You can't help getting attached to them, and to the time and the subject. I loved writing about Ferdinand de Lesseps. I loved writing about John Stevens, the Panama Canal engineer. And Harry Truman. I've been fortunate in my subjects.

Interviewer: What happened to your biography of Picasso?

McCullough: I quit. I didn't like him. I thought I would do him as an event, the Krakatoa of art. He changed the way we see, he changed the imagery of our time. But then I realized that strictly in terms of what would work for me, his wasn't an interesting life. There's an old writer's adage: keep your hero in trouble. With Truman, for instance, that's never a problem, because he's always in trouble. Picasso, on the other hand, was immediately successful. Except for his painting and his love affairs, he lived a prosaic life. He was a communist, which presumably would be somewhat interesting, but during the Nazi occupation of Paris, he seems to have been mainly concerned with his tomato plants. And then his son chains himself to the gate outside trying to get his father's attention; Picasso calls the police to have him taken away. He was an awful man. I don't think you have to love your subject—initially you shouldn't—but it's something like picking a roommate. After all, you're going to be with that person every day, maybe for years, and why subject yourself to someone you have no respect for, or outright don't like?

Interviewer: You thought at one point of becoming a painter yourself, when studying portraiture at Yale.

McCullough: The training I had in drawing and painting has been of great benefit. Drawing is learning to see, and so is writing. It's also an exercise in composition, as writing is, though in writing it's called form.

Growing up in Pittsburgh I went to a wonderful public school where the arts were given as much attention as standard subjects like math and history. We had art and music every day. We were taken to museums and steel mills. I had excellent teachers both in grade school and high school. Most of us are lucky if we have two or three teachers who change our lives, and I had several, especially Vincent Scully, who taught art and architecture at Yale. He taught us to see, to think about spaces, to pay attention to what the buildings were saying, and to think about what the alternatives were, what might have been built that wasn't. And few men I've known have such a great understanding of America. I also took Daily Themes at Yale, Robert Penn Warren's writing course. Every morning at eight thirty you had to slide a sheet of original prose under the professor's door, and if you didn't, you got a zero. There was no kidding about it. It taught us discipline to produce.

The hardest thing with writing is to make it look effortless. It's true of everything that's done well. People see a performer or an artist or a carpenter and they think, Well, that looks easy. Little do they know.

I get a bit impatient with people who talk about all the trials and the pain and loneliness of being a writer. That's not been my experience. I love the work; I would pay to do what I do. That's not to say it's easy, but I don't think ease and pleasure are necessarily synonymous. I like it in part because it *is* hard. And because I don't know how it's going to come out.

Interviewer: What was it like growing up in Pittsburgh?

McCullough: I was very fortunate to have been raised there. We lived in a very nice residential section of the city, but you could smell the coal smoke and hear the trains at night. I was a young boy during the Second World War, when the mills were going full blast, and at night you would see the sky pulsing red from the furnaces going off. It was highly dramatic. In school we were told that the industry of our city was winning the war. We were made to feel we were part of a great world event. We went house to house with wagons collecting scrap metal and bacon fat for the war effort. There were air-raid warnings, sirens, and blackouts. And there sure wasn't any smoke control. Nobody painted a house white; it would be gray in a couple of months. When you put your window down in the morning, the sill would be covered with what looked like black sand—soot from the mills.

A big part of life for me was the Carnegie Museum Library complex, a natural history museum, art museum, library, and concert hall, all under one roof. The building itself conveyed the idea that all these things went together, there were no dividers. You walked from the library into the big hall with a plaster model of the Parthenon and the façades of great buildings from Europe. Around the corner were birds and dinosaurs. Upstairs were the paintings from the permanent collections and visiting exhibitions.

As a kid, twelve years old or so, I could get on the streetcar and go by myself, go see the paintings of Andrew Wyeth and Edward Hopper, go to the library. The architect Louis Kahn said a great city ought to be place where a young person gets an idea of what he might like to do with his life. Well, I certainly did in Pittsburgh. Willa Cather wrote her first stories right near where I grew up. Dreiser lived in Pittsburgh. Stephen Foster was a native son. There were the great musical traditions of the Czechs and Germans and Poles of Pittsburgh. Everybody talks about diversity now. If you were a kid riding the streetcars in Pittsburgh in 1945, you knew about diversity. You heard three or four languages being spoken. You smelled the garlic. You saw the foreign newspapers.

The combination of first-rate public schools and the freedom we had to explore the city on our own—*unsupervised*—well, it was great. I loved growing up there. But I had never seen the ocean, and I think most of all, I wanted to get to New York. Maybe it was seeing so many movies.

HISTORY MATTERS

Interviewer: Could you tell us a little more about the Thomas Jefferson–John Adams book you're working on now?

McCullough: It's about John and Abigail Adams, and to a degree about Jefferson, too. It began as a book about Jefferson and Adams. My plan was to maintain a balance between them, give them each equal time, so to speak. But once under way, I realized it was Adams I wanted to write about, and Abigail as well, most emphatically. I don't think I've ever had better material to work with. First of all, Jefferson and Adams were completely different. In every way. Physically, Adams was short and stout, Jefferson, tall and thin. Adams loved to talk, Jefferson was often ill at ease expressing himself in front of others. Adams loved to argue, Jefferson would never get into an argument with anybody. He didn't want any contention. Abigail was very important to Adams. Their marriage was so interesting. The exchange of ideas, the sentiment and devotion and grief and uncertainty that fill their correspondence are the real thing and nearly always vividly expressed. Because they were separated for so many years, the volume of letters between them is exceptional. Abigail was as learned as any man of her time, and she could write like an angel. And Adams kept a diary. When I read Abigail's letters, I wonder how she ever had time to write them. She was raising a family with four children, running the farm without her husband there; it was nip and tuck whether she could make a go of it financially; she had sickness to contend with, plagues, waves of smallpox and epidemic dysentery that swept through Braintree. How did John Adams have time to write his letters, and keep the diaries? If they'd done nothing else but write what they did, you'd say to yourself, How did they do it? And remember they were writing by candlelight, with a quill

- 47 -

pen, they probably had their teeth hurting because there was no dentistry as we know it. They were probably getting over some recent attack of jaundice or whatever else was epidemic at the time. It's very humbling. You can't help but say hats off to them.

Interviewer: Do you know what your next book will be?

McCullough: No, I probably won't know until I finish the present book. It could result from something I'm writing now, or somebody's chance remark, or something Rosalee and I see while traveling. I'm very interested in the Dome of Santa Maria del Fiore in Florence. I'm fascinated by Brunelleschi and all that was going on in Florence in those years. I love mysteries, and the dome is one. It's still not known how they built it. Yet there it is, built before Columbus sailed.

I'm often asked which is my favorite book, and it's always the same: the one I'm working on. And I feel that now. I really look forward to going out there tomorrow morning and working on chapter three. The time will fly.

—Elizabeth Gaffney, Ben Howe

PART TWO

FIGURES IN A LANDSCAPE

THOMAS EAKINS

For four years in the 1980s, DMcC was the host of the widely acclaimed, Emmy Award–winning PBS series Smithsonian World. *The magazine-format documentary program covered subjects, from across the country and around the world, in science, history, and art. A 1985 episode entitled "Heroes and the Test of Time" explored the life and work of artist Thomas Eakins. DMcC wrote this essay prior to the broadcast.*

He describes the kinds of people Eakins was interested in painting: "The qualities they had in common were self-discipline, high purpose, and high performance achieved through rigorous training, hard work, and continued study. They were people to be taken seriously, doing work of value to society." DMcC could have been describing the people he chose to write about. And perhaps more important, he could be describing himself.

The great American artist Thomas Eakins was fifty-two by the time he was given his first one-man show. Nor would he ever have another while he lived. In his whole career, beginning just after the Civil War, when he returned to Philadelphia after three years of study in France, to the time of his death in 1916, he sold a grand total of just twenty paintings. The best known of his rowing pictures, for example, *Max Schmitt in a Single Scull*, done in 1871 when Eakins was twenty-six, found no buyer until purchased by New York's Metropolitan Museum a generation after his death, in 1934. In all his career, not one author or critic thought enough of Eakins or his work to write even a single magazine article about him.

Yet if Eakins was a comparative nobody in his lifetime, he is a huge somebody today. His giant medical drama, *The Gross Clinic*, his largest, most ambitious undertaking, is spoken of now by many art historians as the American masterpiece of the nineteenth century, possibly the greatest painting by an American ever. The portraits he did, often so disappointing to sitters who hoped to be flattered by the painter, are seen in our day as works of surpassing range and power. Of Eakins's small study of his wife, a picture measuring only sixteen by twenty inches, Abram Lerner, the founding director of the Hirshhorn Museum in Washington, says it ranks with the most penetrating psychological portraits of all time. If the Hirshhorn Museum were ever on fire and he could rescue just one painting, says Lerner, that of Susan MacDowell Eakins would be it.

But what gives Eakins added interest and significance is the subject matter he chose—most especially *whom* he painted, for they stand in telling contrast to those who usually rate popular attention, and in our own time more even than his.

Who really matters to society? he seems to be asking us to consider. Whose lives are being lived in order to matter? Whom should we take seriously? What qualities of self-discipline and character do we wish to honor with fame? Who ought to be the heroes of our modern times, if we truly mean business about the ideal of human progress?

By Eakins's lights, we are wasting a great deal of time and attention on the wrong people. Had there been a *People* magazine then, few of those he chose to celebrate on canvas would have figured in its pages. Indeed, he stood for just about everything our present fame industry does not. Our prevailing mode of instant celebrity, based as it so often is on little or no ability or hard-won achievement of any real consequence, would have been wholly uninteresting to him. Or outright repellent. And it's not simply that we have instant celebrity—overnight superstars and the rest, the way we have instant soup or "fast, fast, fast" relief for whatever ails us—but that we have throwaway celebrity as well. The civilization that has brought us Styrofoam cups and disposable razors, diapers, and marriages has also provided the disposable celebrity. All very up-to-date and handy, and with it, of course, comes the implicit understanding that what we throw away has no actual value anyway.

Eakins by contrast was painting not for the moment, or even for the span of his own generation. As the best of the architects and engineers of that often gaudy but purposeful era—the Roeblings, H. H. Richardson, Louis Sullivan—were building things to last, so Eakins saw his paintings as an enduring historical record. Throughout his career he painted little other than portraits, which in itself set him off from the fashionable mainstream. But of the more than two hundred portraits he painted, only twenty-five were commissioned. All his other subjects were asked by Eakins to sit for him. In other words, he was conferring his own kind of homage, painting his own gallery of achievement. As art historian Elizabeth Johns writes in her superb book, *Thomas Eakins: The Heroism of Modern Life*, "For him the human being was central to art—but not just any man or woman with an interesting face; rather he sought the person who in his full intellectual, aesthetic, and athletic power was definitive of the best of his times."

The qualities they had in common were self-discipline, high purpose, and high performance achieved through rigorous training, hard work, and continued study. They were people to be taken seriously, doing work of value to society. They were physicians, scholars, scientists, churchmen, musicians, artists, writers. Comparatively few were successful in a worldly way. A large number, whatever their profession, were also dedicated teachers, as was Eakins himself. It wasn't enough to excel in one's work, Eakins held, but essential to teach others also, to pass the torch.

Most came from humble origins and were thus self-made. With few exceptions, they were people he knew personally in and about Philadelphia, and whose work he also knew. The beautiful people of his day, the rich, the wheeler dealers, the socially important, did not qualify. Nor did politicians, with the exception of the president of the United States, Rutherford B. Hayes, one of Eakins's few commissions. The power elite of the community is notably absent. Nobody he chose to paint was the sort to have had a press agent.

The first prominent Philadelphian to sit was Benjamin H. Rand, professor of chemistry at the Jefferson Medical College, who is shown at his desk with books and microscope. Others who followed included Dr. D. Hayes Agnew, noted surgeon and professor of surgery and anatomy at the University of Pennsylvania, a man of fine physique and exceptional physical endurance (in later life Agnew once remarked that he never knew what it was to be tired); and Archbishop James Frederick Wood, a convert to Catholicism, a former banker, an energetic administrator and educator, who became the first archbishop of Philadelphia. Eakins painted the celebrated anthropologist Frank Hamilton Cushing, who had lived for years among the Zuni Indians, and Walt Whitman, who was living out his final years in nearby Camden, New Jersey, his poetry largely neglected by the public.

The Concert Singer, among the most haunting of Eakins's portraits, is of contralto Weda Cook, an accomplished, well-loved Philadelphia performer. *The Cello Player* is Rudolf Hennig, a German immigrant, teacher, and much-acclaimed soloist. And Eakins's rowers, like the musicians, were also well known locally—heroes with a Philadelphia following. Max Schmitt, a boyhood friend, was an amateur rower but champion of the single sculls on the Schuylkill River, and like all Eakins's champions, whether in medicine, music, the arts, Schmitt had attained his standing through extraordinary dedication. Moreover, rowing was a sport where you won by total concentration on your own task, your own performance, not the other fellow's. As Elizabeth Johns writes, the rower "never set his stroke by that of a competitor but rowed according to his own, or his crew's own, steady discipline." It was how Eakins, himself a rower and natural athlete, approached his whole life's work and an attitude he admired always in others.

He painted no everyday people, as, say, Winslow Homer did. Even those of his own family or intimate friends whom he chose to immortalize were people of genuine distinction in his eyes. For instance, he regarded his wife, Susan, as the most gifted woman painter of the day.

But the figure who loomed largest in Eakins's estimate, exemplifying better than anyone his idea of a hero worthy of acclaim, was Dr. Samuel David Gross, the pioneer physician and teacher who dominates the drama of *The Gross Clinic*. He was the most eminent American surgeon of the nineteenth century, the crown jewel of the faculty at Philadelphia's Jefferson Medical College, and everything, in Eakins's view, that democracy and the march of modern science ought to give rise to in the way of a citizen.

Born on a small Pennsylvania farm, Gross had fixed on his career in boyhood; taught himself Greek, Latin, mathematics; and became one of the earliest students at Jefferson. In his thirties he wrote the first book in English to present pathological anatomy in any kind of systematic fashion. His beautifully written two-volume *A System of Surgery* was the surgical bible of the day and went through six editions. He founded the Pathological Society of Philadelphia and the Philadelphia Academy of Surgery and presided over the International Medical Congress in 1876, at the time of the Centennial Exhibition in Philadelphia. His brilliant exposition and commanding presence as a teacher were legendary. In the words of one biographical sketch, "It is probable that no finer mind was ever devoted to the art and science of surgery."

Eakins knew Gross from firsthand experience. A lifelong student of anatomy himself, Eakins had attended many a Gross clinic. And in his great canvas Eakins portrays the surgeon-teacher in the midst of one of his famous performances in the Jefferson amphitheater, as he and a surgical team are removing a diseased thigh bone. There is much blood—indeed, the painting was turned down for the enormous art exhibit at the Centennial because it was considered too unpleasant—but Eakins has made the focus of his drama the great leonine head of Gross. The light is on the cranium, seat of the mind.

"Strain your brain more than your eye," Eakins would tell his own students at the Pennsylvania Academy of the Fine Arts, where he had established the most rigorous curriculum of any art school in the nation. "A few hours' intelligent study is better than a whole day of thoughtless plodding." The main thing was to know what you were about. "Did you see those charcoal drawings by Degas?" he once remarked to a student. "I saw one of a ballet girl putting on her tights. He had that wriggle of the foot. The action was good. It was done with a few strokes of charcoal. That fellow knew what he was about."

And Professor Rand, the chemist; Agnew, the surgeon; Archbishop Wood; anthropologist Cushing; contralto Cook; cellist Hennig; Max Schmitt; Susan MacDowell Eakins; and Samuel David Gross, they, too, knew what they were about.

They all made or contributed something of value to the community—knowledge, healing skill, music, art, and beyond that and of such inestimable value, their example. Dr. Gross, on hearing applause as he entered the surgical amphitheater to address a new class of students, told them he wanted no more of that. "There is something awfully solemn in a profession which deals with life and death," he said, "and I desire at the very threshold of this course of lectures to impress upon your minds its sacred and responsible character."

Most important, Eakins, as a fellow member of the community, was in a position to judge. He was never conferring acclaim from some distant editorial mountaintop. In building his pantheon, no less than in his work as a painter, he knew what he was about.

Further, he had no deadlines to meet, no quotas to fill. Imagine trying to fill the pages of almost any of our weekly magazines or all those early morning talk show hours with new faces, new movers and shakers, and "important" new talents, day after day after day without ever any letup.

Eakins himself was wholly without affectation, a strenuous worker, a fervent lowercase democrat. His world was his work, his students (to whom he was a model of integrity), his wife, his city, a small circle of friends, his home at 1729 Mount Vernon Street where he had lived as a boy and where he died. He was passionately fond of the outdoors. He was fascinated by mathematics and photography. He never stopped learning. In all, he was very like those he most admired, and his persistence in the face of critical scorn or indifference is testimony to one further quality common to those he celebrated on canvas: courage. To take up a scalpel to save a life in that comparatively primitive age of medicine was no work for the fainthearted. In most every portrait Eakins painted, one feels a brave if lonely resolution in the face of time and mortality. Life itself, he seems to be saying, is an act of courage.

If he were alive today, one might ask, Whom would he be painting? My guess is they would be the very same kinds of people in much the same professions and almost certainly they would be Philadelphians, since he never wanted to live or work anywhere else.

Possibly he wanted applause no more than had Dr. Gross. His wife said he did not care to be written about, and as late as 1929, she was sure his work would never be popular. Walt Whitman, soon after he and Eakins met, concluded Eakins was "no usual man." He thought Eakins's portrait of him the best yet. Another time Whitman observed, "Eakins is not a painter, he is a force." Evidently it took one to know one. And such recognition from Whitman would have meant more than any amount of ordinary fanfare.

Once, given the chance to blow his own horn, when asked to provide a biographical sketch of himself, Eakins put down the date of his birth, plus a few words on his ancestry, the names of his teachers in France, and brief mention of his own teaching career. Then he wrote, "For the public, I believe my life is all in my work."

HARRIET BEECHER STOWE IN PARIS

DMcC was exhilarated when his subjects surprised him—when they said or did things that were unexpected. Both Wright brothers surprised him again and again, as did Abigail Adams, Thomas Jefferson, Katharine Wright, Theodore Roosevelt, and Harry Truman. The list goes on and on.

Harriet Beecher Stowe, the author of Uncle Tom's Cabin, *was a character of interest for DMcC for decades. In 1973, he wrote an essay called "The Unexpected Mrs. Stowe." A decade later, he revisited her to include that essay in his book* Brave Companions. *When he began working on* The Greater Journey, *in 2007, he didn't imagine he'd find Harriet Beecher Stowe—the little woman with all those children, writing by hand in a damp New England kitchen—at the Louvre. But there she was in Paris, captivated by Théodore Géricault's* The Raft of the Medusa.

In 1852, a new novel titled *Uncle Tom's Cabin* by an unknown author from Maine caused the greatest stir of anything published in America since Thomas Paine's *Common Sense*. In the first year, three hundred thousand copies were sold in the United States alone. By the spring of 1853, the book had become a sensation in Britain as well, and its author, Harriet Beecher Stowe, unknown no longer, was on her way to England in the "hope of doing good" for the cause against slavery, as she told her friend Senator Charles Sumner of Massachusetts.

In Britain, *Uncle Tom's Cabin* was acclaimed for accomplishing greater good for humanity than any other book of fiction. Over half a million British women had signed a petition against slavery. In Paris, where the Stowes were also headed, publishers were still scrambling to finish translations, but the novelist George Sand, writing in *La Presse*, had already called Mrs. Stowe "a saint. Yes—a saint!"

Traveling with her were her husband, the preacher-scholar Calvin Stowe; her younger brother Charles Beecher, also a preacher; and three of her in-laws but none of her six children. They crossed on the steamship *Canada*, and for Hatty, as she was known in the family, it was, at age forty-one, her first time at sea.

The author's British tour was long and exhausting. Having taken no part in the antislavery movement prior to writing her book, she suddenly found herself the most influential voice speaking on behalf of the enslaved people of America. From the day her ship docked at Liverpool, crowds awaited her at every stop of the tour through England and Scotland. Husband Calvin was so undone by it all that he gave up and went home.

By the time Hatty reached Paris, in the first week of June, she craved only some peace and privacy and wanted her presence in the city kept as quiet as possible. Rather than staying at one of the fashionable hotels, she moved into a private mansion on the narrow rue de Verneuil in the Faubourg Saint-Germain, as the guest of an American friend, Maria Weston Chapman, known as "the soul" of the Boston Female Anti-Slavery Society.

"At last I have come into a dreamland," Hatty wrote. "I am released from care. I am unknown, unknowing."

With her time all her own, she used it to see everything possible, starting the next day, a Sunday, with church service at the Madeleine, her first "Romish" service ever. She usually went accompanied by her brother Charles, whose energetic, good-humored companionship she relished. For nearly three weeks she moved about Paris unnoticed, a small, fragile-looking woman of no apparent importance—"a little bit of a woman," as she said, "about as thin and dry as a pinch of snuff, never very much to look at in my best days."

She was tireless and saw everything that so many Americans had seen before her but took time to look hard and to think about what she saw. Hatty was a natural "observer," wrote Charles, "always looking around on everything." And for all that others had had to say on the same subjects, there was a freshness, an originality, in what she wrote.

She loved Paris at once. She needed no coaching, no interlude in which to acclimate herself. She felt immediately at home, and better just for being among the people. "My spirits always rise when I get among the French."

The days were unseasonably warm, the temperature eighty degrees in the shade, as she recorded in her journal, describing the pleasure of sitting beneath the trees in the Garden of the Tuileries, observing the human show.

> Whole families come, locking up their door, bringing the baby, work, dinner, or lunch, take a certain number of chairs and spend the day. As far as the eye can reach, you see a multitude seated, as if in church, with other multitudes moving to and fro, while boys and girls without number are frolicking, racing, playing ball, driving hoop, etc., but contriving to do it without making a hideous racket

How French children were taught to play and enjoy themselves without disturbing everyone else was a mystery to her.

> There were gray-headed old men and women, and invalids. And there were beautiful demoiselles working worsted, embroidery, sewing; men reading papers, and, in fact, people doing everything they would do in their own parlors. All were graceful, kind, and obliging; not a word nor an act of impoliteness or indecency.

No wonder the French adore Paris, she thought.

Pausing for an ice at a garden café at the Palais-Royal after a long day, she was delighted to find so many others doing the same. No one recognized the plain little American or paid her any attention—just as she wished.

Another day, after climbing with Charles up the spiral staircase to the top of the Arc de Triomphe, she made no mention of the nearly three hundred steps, only the thrill of the view. But whatever the vantage point, she refused to let slip from her mind how much might lay out of sight. "All is vivacity, gracefulness, and sparkle to the eye, but, ah, what fires are smoldering below."

Seeing Louis Napoleon Bonaparte, who had recently declared himself Emperor Napoleon III, and his wife, Eugénie, ride by in their carriage on the boulevard des Italiens, Hatty thought he looked stiff and homely, she beautiful but sad.

Until the evening her host Maria Chapman held one of her salons on the rue de Verneuil, setting out cake and tea for a gathering of Parisian friends, neither Hatty nor Charles had ventured to say much in French. Charles decided to throw caution to the winds and "talked away, right and left, and right and wrong, too," as he wrote, "a perfect steeple chase, jumping over ditches and hedges, genders and cases . . . nouns, adjectives, and terminations of all sorts." The guests were amazed and delighted, as was his sister. "Poor Hatty!" he wrote. "She could not talk French, except to say, '*Oui, madame. Non, monsieur.*'"

The attention paid to her at this and other small gatherings by those who knew who she was, was "very touching," Charles thought. "She is made to feel perfectly free. . . . And the regard felt for her is manifested in a way . . . so considerate that she is rather *strengthened* by it than exhausted."

What was the mysterious allure of Paris? she wondered. What was its hold on the heart and imagination? Surely the "life artery" was the ever-flowing Seine, she mused one day when crossing the Pont d'Austerlitz. The years she had spent in her twenties and early thirties in Cincinnati, living in the presence of the Ohio and later writing about it in her book, had given her a strong inner sense of the river as a divider, an open highway, a measure of the turning of the seasons, of life. But the Seine, embellished with such bridges and show of monumental architecture, was like no river she had ever known. "And there is no scene like this, as I gaze upward and downward, comprehending in a glance the immense panorama of art and architecture—life, motion, enterprise, pleasure, pomp, and power."

> As the instinct of the true Parisienne teaches her the mystery of setting off the graces of her person by the fascinations of dress, so the instinct of the nation to set off the city by the fascinations of architecture and embellishment.

Gazing upward within the Cathedral of Notre-Dame, Hatty felt a "sublimity" she found impossible to analyze or express. It was a long way from the kitchen table in Brunswick, Maine, where she had written *Uncle Tom's Cabin*, a baby in a clothes basket at her feet.

She had become increasingly interested in art. So the Louvre occupied the greater part of her time. She knew nothing of the "rules of painting," as she said, but confident in what she knew of the art of literature, she compared the painters who most strongly appealed to her to one or another of her favorite writers. Rembrandt struck her as very like Hawthorne, for example.

> He chooses simple and everyday objects, and so arranges light and shadow as to give them a somber richness and a mysterious gloom. *The House of Seven Gables* is a succession of Rembrandt pictures done in words instead of oils. Now this pleases us because our life really is a haunted one. The simplest thing in it *is* a mystery, the invisible world always lies round us like a shadow....

There were no paintings in the museum to which she returned as often as those by Rembrandt. Rubens—"the great, joyous, full-souled, all-powerful Rubens!"—whom she loved no less, was like Shakespeare, she decided. Yet Rubens bothered her. He was full of "triumphant, abounding life, disgusting and pleasing, making me laugh and making me angry, defying me to dislike him."

> Like Shakespeare, he forces you to accept and forgive a thousand excesses, and uses his own faults as musicians use discords only to enhance the perfection of harmony. There certainly is some use even in defects. A faultless style sends you to sleep. Defects rouse and excite sensibility to seek and appreciate excellences.

Walking back and forth the length of the Grande Galerie, pausing to look at pictures from a distance and up close, she found few "glorious enough to seize and control my whole being." Too many artists "painted with dry eyes and cool hearts," she thought, "thinking only of mixing their colors and the jugglery of their art, thinking little of heroes, faith, love, or immortality."

For the large works of Jacques-Louis David hanging with other French paintings in the Salon Carré, she had little use. The problem with David was that he had neither heart nor soul. His paintings were but the "driest imitation" of the classics.

She saw French painting as representative of the "great difficulty and danger" of French life in general:

> ... that passion for the outward and visible, which all their education, all arrangements of their social life, everything in their art and literature, tends continually to cultivate and increase. Hence, they have become the leaders of the world in what I should call the minor artistics—all those particulars which render life beautiful. Hence there are more pretty pictures and popular lithographs from France than from any other country in the world, but it produces very little of the deepest and highest style of art.

But there was one stunning exception, she was quick to concede, *The Raft of the Medusa*, the tremendous (16 by 23½ feet) dark canvas by Théodore Géricault showing the tragic victims of an 1816 disaster, when the ship *Medusa* went aground off the coast of Senegal. There are no heroes on the crude raft in Géricault's wild, dark, unforgiving sea. At least two of the figures in the foreground are already dead. Those still alive cling to one another, and the whole thrust of the pyramid of their bodies is to the upper right-hand corner, where the strongest of the living, a black man, waves a shirt or rag toward one dim semblance of hope, the mere speck of a ship on the far horizon.

If any great work in the Louvre had the power to "seize and control" her whole being, she wrote, it was this. She spent a full hour in front of it.

> I gazed until all surrounding objects disappeared, and I was alone in the wide Atlantic. Those transparent emerald waves are no fiction. They leap madly, hungering for their prey. That distended sail is filled with the lurid air. The dead man's foot hangs off in the seething brine a stark reality. What a fixed gaze of despair in that father's stony eye! What a group of deathly living ones around that frail mast, while one with intense eagerness flutters a signal to some far-described bark! Coleridge's Ancient Mariner has no colors more fearfully faithful to his theme. . . . And there is no voice that can summon the distant flying sail!

Here was the work of a man "who had not seen human life and suffering merely on the outside but had felt in the very depths of his soul the surging and earthquake of those mysteries of passion and suffering which underlie our whole existence in this world." She was sure no more powerful piece had ever been painted. It was as though this one picture had been worth the whole trip to France.

After not quite three weeks, she and her party were on their way to the Swiss Alps and Germany but soon were back in Paris for a longer stay. She had been thinking about the human need for beauty and how during her childhood in Connecticut she had been starved for that side of life. She felt she had been senselessly, cruelly cheated. "With all New England's earnestness and practical efficiency, there is a long withering of the soul's more ethereal part—a crushing out of the beautiful—which is horrible."

> Children are born there with a sense of beauty equally delicate with any in the world in whom it dies a lingering death of smothered desire and pining, weary starvation. I know because I have felt it.

It was a severe indictment of her own upbringing, indeed of American life, and not until she came to Paris had it struck her so emphatically.

More important was the realization that the beauty of Paris was not just one of the pleasures of the city, but it possessed a magically curative power to bring one's own sense of beauty back to life. "One in whom this sense had long been repressed, in coming into Paris, feels a rustling and a waking within him, as if the soul were crying to unfold her wings." Instead of scorning the lighthearted, beauty-loving French, she decided, Americans ought to recognize how much was to be learned from them.

A CONVERSATION ABOUT GEORGE

DMcC gave thousands of speeches over the course of his career, and the vast majority, such as "A Conversation About George," were delivered without notes, each tailored to the specific audience before him. He always preferred a lavalier microphone because it gave him the freedom to walk about the stage. Walking helped him to think, he believed, and it also allowed the audience to know he was speaking extemporaneously. Working with a transcription, we made some minor adjustments in this piece for clarity. Naturally, DMcC's speaking and writing were not identical.

Here is DMcC speaking at the Library of Congress in 1999. He came to believe that George Washington was the greatest American ever.

We can't turn our backs on people like George Washington. We can't take them for granted. We can't take them for granted as human beings and as figures in our history. To be indifferent to history isn't just to be ignorant, it's often to be rude, to show a form of ingratitude. And ingratitude was one of the human failings that George Washington, as it happens, disliked intensely. Our gratitude to George Washington should be beyond measure and to have had that particular man with his integrity, his courage, his decency, his stability, his sense of duty to the common good, as our first president is almost miraculous.

And to think who he had in his cabinet—the people of such stature coming forth out of a tiny country. We had about two and a half million people in the whole country at the time of the Revolutionary War. And what people fail to understand is how dark—how unlikely—seemed the chances of American success in the Revolutionary War.

If you remember the play Thornton Wilder's *Our Town*, the character Emily says at the end of the play—that wonderful character, Emily—that the hardest thing in life is to realize it while it's happening to you. And that's very true of history. We assume that everybody who's involved in historic events is caught up in the fact that they are involved in an historic event. One of my favorite moments in the life of George Washington took place when he was sixteen years old. He'd gone for the first time away from home up to Ashby Gap, which is right where the little town of Paris, Virginia, is—where Route 17 goes through the gap. And George had never been away from home. He was out in real wilderness. And they went through the gap on March 12, Sunday, 1748; and they saw, he saw, the Shenandoah Valley for the first time. There was this vast paradise—the future, the West, the Blue Ridge Mountains beyond. It was easily one of the most spectacular vantage points both physically and, if you will, metaphysically for this historic character—sixteen-year-old George—to have ever been in. And that night in his little diary, he wrote, "Nothing remarkable happened." I loved him from that point on. I thought, This is terrific.

How can we understand somebody from the past—how do you reach these people, these distant people, who lived in a very different time? You cannot assume that because an onion tasted the same to them or the stars were in the same configuration, that they were just like we are. They weren't just like we are, because they lived in a different time. And one of the ways you try to understand them, if you're struggling to write biography or history, is to read what people at the time said about them. Benjamin Latrobe, the architect, said Washington has something uncommonly majestic and commanding in his walk, his address, his figure, and his countenance. So Latrobe, the architect, is looking at the architecture of this man. And he's very impressed by this physical presence of this large man—six foot two—well over 180 pounds, 200 pounds when he was older. Jefferson equally characteristically is looking at the mind. He says his mind was great and powerful without being of the very first order. His penetration strong, though not so acute as that of a Newton, Bacon, or Locke. Well, that's sort of the eighteenth-century way of saying he was no Einstein. And as far as Jefferson saw, no judgment was sounder. It was slow in operation, little-sighted by invention or imagination, but sure in conclusion. Gilbert Stuart of course, was looking at the face. And he said that, surprisingly, all his features were indicative of the most ungovernable passions. You always hear about how cold George Washington was—how aloof—how removed. He didn't smile very much. He didn't talk very much. But Gilbert Stuart saw these ungovernable passions, and "had he been born in the forest," he said, "he would have been the fiercest man among the savage tribes." Stuart sensed in Washington a very different man from cold, unapproachable George Washington. Lafayette, who was more like a son to George Washington and who, of course, was a soldier, saw him as a soldier. And he said, "Had he been a common soldier, he would have been the bravest in the ranks." He was a very brave man—very courageous man. And that is essential to understanding who he was and his character. Then, of course, famously, there is the great line of Henry Lee—"Light-Horse Harry Lee"—at one of the many orations after Washington's death who called him "first in war, first in peace, first in the hearts of his countrymen." And it's still true today.

And then there was the press. Ah, the press. He was denounced as pompous, vainglorious, a spendthrift. He was compared to Oliver Cromwell. He was called a traitor. And no less than the apostle of liberty than Thomas Paine called him treacherous in private friendship and a hypocrite in public life. Almost anything that you can think of that's been said about political leaders in our time was said about those political leaders in that time.

In many ways, it was John Adams who saw the strength in Washington and the importance of Washington the earliest. After all, it was John Adams who put Washington's name in nomination to command the Continental army at Philadelphia in 1776, sending a Virginian to Boston to command a New England army. It was the first important, political, military, psychological, symbolic gesture at union between these two vastly different worlds of the North and the South.

WASHINGTON WAS BORN IN Westmoreland County, Virginia, in 1732. He died at the age of sixty-seven in 1799—two hundred years ago this year. Our capital city was named for him. So were 121 other cities and towns across the country. There's a state, seven mountains, ten lakes, thirty-two counties, and nine colleges named for George Washington. And, of course, there's the Washington Monument, which is our greatest public work of abstract sculpture. And there is the greatest, in my view, equestrian statue in America, which is the equestrian figure of George Washington by the brilliant sculptor Thomas Ball, which stands at the opening of the Public Garden in Boston. Washington has been on our money since our money was first printed. And his visage, his face, I've read, appears on no less than three hundred different postage stamps in more than fifty nations. Whether he truly slept in as many places as he's supposed to have is not for me to say. In all, there have been more than three thousand books about George Washington. He ranks up there with Lincoln and Napoleon as one of the most written-about subjects of all.

The eighteenth century gave us *The Decline and Fall of the Roman Empire*, Houdon's great marble portrait of Washington, *Tristram Shandy*, Voltaire, Rousseau, the Constitution of the Commonwealth of Massachusetts, which is the oldest written constitution still in operation in the world and which predates the national Constitution by about ten years—and, of course, Adam Smith's *Wealth of Nations*. It was a protean, exciting, intellectually stimulating time such as the world had never seen. And we all still live as its benefactors in one way or another. But the most important event of the eighteenth century was the advent of the United States of America—without any question.

Nothing in the past had to happen the way it happened. That's the hardest thing to convey in writing history or teaching history—that nothing had to happen the way it happened. Any event, any sequence of events could have gone differently for any number of different reasons at any point, any way, anywhere along the line. We did not necessarily have to have a George Washington, but it happened.

There is another point I feel very strongly about, and that is this fiction of a simpler past. You see some of these wizards on television talking about how things are so difficult and troublesome today; and then somebody will bring up some time in the past and they'll say, "Oh yes, but that was a simpler time." There was no simpler time. I often think of those troops at night—ragged, forlorn, pathetic troops of Washington's crossing the Delaware in the snow and the ice to attack on Christmas Eve, Christmas night, the Hessians, the toughest of troops in the world, to attack them, this little spindly army—tramping along in the dark and the freezing cold. Some of them didn't even have shoes. And maybe one turns to the other and says, "Yes, but at least we live in a simpler time." It was a very complicated time. It was a very dangerous time. And you had to have a lot of stamina. You had to have a sense of purpose just to get through life very often, let alone in time of war.

Let me tell you just a little bit, in my view, what George Washington was not. He was not an easy oratorical virtuoso. He was not glib. He was not highly educated. He's surrounded by Jefferson, Adams, Hamilton, Madison—all very educated people. He has relatively little formal school at all. He was not a great military genius. He made some classic blunders as a general in the Revolutionary War. He was not a natural-born politician. He was not—definitely not—a party man. And he was not clearly destined for greatness from the beginning. He wasn't somebody that you could spot right away: He's the one. Do you realize when he took command of the Continental army in 1775 at Boston, he'd never commanded anything larger than a regiment in his life? He was a farmer. He was not a professional career soldier. He was not easy to know. He never was easy to know. And he didn't want to be easy to know, because he knew how easily one could attract friends and how often he wanted to get rid of some of those friends. So he chose his friends very carefully—with his heart. And once you were his friend, that was it forever. He never learned how to flatter. He was not untrustworthy, and he was not a hypocrite.

He was always prompt, and he expected others to be, too. He was always well and appropriately dressed. He was always courteous. He was always, until later years, highly ambitious in a good, healthy way. He was supremely, uncommonly courageous. That cannot be overstressed. And as his great biographer, Douglas Southall Freeman, wrote, "He always kept his head under the most adverse, complicated, and trying conditions." But most of all, he was a leader. I think that's the essence of George Washington. He was a leader, and he could inspire people to do things beyond what they thought they had the capacity to do. And that's a direct, personal thing. He knew how to lead men, and after the war, he knew how to lead the country.

In my view, one of the most astute of all observers of George Washington, one of the most astute observers of that whole era, that whole period in our nation's life, and one of the wisest of all Americans ever was Abigail Adams. And what she wrote about George Washington is as perceptive as almost anything to be found. Here's some of what she said: "He is polite with dignity, affable without familiarity, distant without haughtiness, grave without austerity, modest, wise, and good." He was a good human being. "There are traits in his character which perfectly fit him for the exalted station he holds." She's writing this in 1790 when Washington is president. "And God grant that he may hold it with the same applause and universal satisfaction for many as it is my firm opinion that no other man could rule over this great people and consolidate them into one mighty empire but he who is set over us now." Again, he is this unifying figure, this Southerner who is a national treasure—a national hero.

For much of the Revolutionary War, Abigail was alone at home in Braintree, Massachusetts, trying to take care of her family—four children, her husband's away at the Continental Congress in Philadelphia. She was snowed in, in the winter of '76–'77. There is a smallpox epidemic and dysentery sweeping through New England. She's trying to make ends meet. She's trying to maintain correspondence with her husband. She's a very brave woman fighting the Revolutionary War in her way as much as anybody else in their ways.

When Washington counterattacks at Trenton, he's been chased, he's been defeated at Brooklyn—the Battle of Long Island—he's been defeated at White Plains, he's had to make an ignominious retreat all the way south across New Jersey, desperate to get across the Delaware, away from the pursuing British Army. His army is down to about four thousand people, from twenty thousand people earlier that summer in his army. And they're underclothed, underfed, and he's across the river and there's every reason in the world to tuck his tail between his legs and go hide in the woods somewhere till it all blew over. But what did he do? He attacked—unbelievable—he attacked, and he attacked at night, and it was successful. Now, this was not a great battle, nor was Princeton, which followed right after. These were engagements. But you cannot overestimate the importance of what that did to the country. And Abigail Adams back in Braintree, Massachusetts, in a house that you could put three of them in this space here, writes in a letter to John, "I am apt to think that our late misfortunes have called out the hidden excellencies of our commander in chief. Affliction is a good man's shining time," she said, quoting her favorite poet, Edward Young. "Affliction is a good man's shining time." He was at his best when things were at their worst, and it gave everybody a lift. So his leadership transcended the battlefield. It transcended the immediate people around him.

IF YOU WERE GOING to look for sort of a defining time in Washington's presidency, I think it's probably the spring and summer of 1794 when there were major crises everywhere. The British were threatening us from Canada. General Wayne—Mad Anthony Wayne—was with the army at Fallen Timbers. There were very serious threats of war with France. John Jay was on his way to England, and then the Whiskey Rebellion broke out in dear old western Pennsylvania. And we had what they called then the insurrection west of the mountains. This was a serious uprising, and what do you do about it? You're a new country. Everything is new. And Washington says, "What may be the consequences of such violent and outrageous proceedings is painful in a high degree even in contemplation? But if the laws are to be so trampled upon with impunity and a minority—a small one, too—is to dictate to the majority, there is an end put at one stroke to Republican government." He handled this crisis, it seemed to me, at his best. He *was* at his best. He was firm. He was principled. He was humane. And he also waited for Congress to give him the power to raise the militia. Something, for example, that Harry Truman did not do with Korea—a mistake. And he marched—he rode at the head of the army. President of the United States in uniform on horseback leading the army west from Philadelphia toward Carlisle, Pennsylvania. This was the commander in chief literally, not figuratively. The symbolism of Washington taking command himself, needless to say, was not lost on the country.

We have, of course, some powerful old stories, myths—call them what you will—about George Washington. Parson Weems's book and the little six-year-old George with his hatchet saying he could not tell a lie. And you may remember that the father says, "Did you do this?" George says, "I did. I cannot tell a lie." And the father says, "Come to my arms, son. Such an act of heroism in my son is worth more than a thousand trees, though their fruits be purest gold." Then there's Washington crossing the Delaware, standing up in the boat, in the great painting which hangs today in the Metropolitan Museum, and still one of the most popular of all paintings in that museum. Now these myths, these stories, are stories. They're not literally true, but they get to the truth about him, which is why they live and why they're valid. He cared about the truth. He was brave—brave enough to face his father with what he'd done. He might not have stood up in that boat—almost certainly he didn't stand up in the boat crossing the Delaware. It's the wrong kind of boat in the painting. The flags are wrong, the uniforms are wrong. It's all wrong, but it's entirely right in that he did cross the Delaware that night under those terrible conditions and he is—in the way the painting is constructed—he is the force that's going to change history forever with his courage.

And then the wooden teeth. The teeth were not wooden. He had terrible trouble with his teeth. They were made as most false teeth were then of ivory or lead or cow teeth or human teeth. They were poorly designed to fit in one's mouth. And what does that tell us? It tells us he suffers the frailties of all human beings—that he was, in fact, vulnerable as a person, as a human. These myths should not be discounted as trivial or childlike. They should be embraced for the reality they remind us of. It is not in mortals to command success, but we'll do more, we'll deserve it.

One of the greatest lines I know: "It is not in mortals to command success, but we'll do more, we'll deserve it." How contrary that line is to all so much of the world we live in and the culture that we live in today where success is all that matters no matter how you get it. This is a completely different ethic, a completely different attitude toward life. It's *deserving* it that's more important than the success. Now, where did that come from? When you read it in Washington's letters, when you read it in John Adams's letters, there are no quotation marks around it. And so, if you're going along and suddenly you run into this sentence, what it means, and it stops you cold; and then you realize they didn't say it. It's a line from Joseph Addison's play *Cato*. They all knew it, and they didn't put quotation marks around it any more than we would put quotation marks around "Well, I'll have to follow the yellow brick road," or something like that. They all knew it. Now, if they knew it, it was in them. Why was this little country—why were these handful of people—how in the world did they have the talent, how in the world did they have the heart to do what they did? I think it's tied up in that idea, and it's very interesting. It turns up again in the twentieth century in a very powerful famous speech given by Winston Churchill. "We cannot guarantee success. We can do better. We can deserve it."

George Washington is the only slave-owning president of the United States who freed his slaves at his death. George Washington was a visionary. He was experimenting. We think of Jefferson as very experimental and inventive. He was; so was Washington. Washington had a gristmill, a sawmill. Washington had a very active and progressive fish farming enterprise at Mount Vernon where in some years it was more profitable than his farms. He also, in the last few years of his life, established a distillery.

He was the real thing. He wasn't a contrivance. He was the authentic thing—the authentic great man, a true American hero, a figure of world importance. If you go into the rotunda at the Capitol, you'll see the paintings—the famous paintings of the great scenes in Washington's life—this man who wouldn't give up, who wouldn't give in, wouldn't give up no matter what, gives up the most important thing of all—power. It's portrayed in the painting in the rotunda. He's turning over the command, the power of the Continental army, to the Congress after the war. No conquering general had ever done that. And when George III heard this was going to happen, he said, "If he does that, he will be the greatest man in the world." And he did, and he was. And in this day of our own when so much is synthetic and contrived and fabricated and false, it's hard for many people to recognize the authentic when they see it or when they read about it.

And that's why it's so important that they be able to go to Mount Vernon and be reminded that a person lived here—not a god—a person, a human being. But he is no apocryphal hero. He was real. To be indifferent to George Washington is to miss the point about who you are, who we are, and how we got to be where we are. We are all in his debt. He was there at the beginning. He won the war. He won the most important war in our history, because without it, there would have been no country as we know it. And he set the standard as president again and again in everything he did. Jefferson was very worried about the Constitution because the president could get in power and stay in power forever. Washington gave the example of two terms. Washington, in almost everything he did, set the example. He was the example. He was truly indispensable. And for those people in that time to have thought that this was the hand of God in the fate and in the liberty of America, for them to have thought that, believed that, was perfectly understandable. To a large degree, he wasn't just there at the beginning. He *was* the beginning. And what infinitely good fortune for the United States of America. We can never know enough about George Washington.

HARRY S. TRUMAN

DMcC worked on his book Truman *for a solid ten years. It is a biography of 996 pages, with 2,986 source notes. He often said, had he known at the outset how much archival material there was at the Truman Library, he wouldn't have had the courage to begin. Then, quickly, he would add how grateful he was for not knowing.*

In the 1990s, his friend Bob Wilson produced a presidential history lecture series, and a book called Character Above All. *This is DMcC's contribution.*

Harry Truman was president of the United States for not quite eight years. Looking back now we see him standing there in the presidential line, all of five foot nine, in a double-breasted suit, between two heroic figures of the century, Franklin Delano Roosevelt and Dwight D. Eisenhower. It's hard to convey today the feeling Americans had about General Eisenhower, the aura of the man, after World War II. He was charismatic, truly, if anyone ever was. Truman was not like that, not glamorous, not photogenic. And from the April afternoon when Truman took office, following the death of Franklin Roosevelt, he would feel the long shadow of Roosevelt, the most colossal figure in the White House in this century. He had none of Roosevelt's gifts—no beautiful speaking voice, no inherited wealth or social standing, no connections. He is the only president of our century who never went to college, and along with his clipped Missouri twang and eyeglasses thick as the bottom of a Coke bottle, he had a Middle Western plainness of manner that, at first glance, made him seem "ordinary."

He had arrived first in Washington in the 1930s as a senator notable mainly for his background in the notorious Pendergast machine of Kansas City. He was of Scotch Irish descent, and like many of Scotch Irish descent—and I know something of this from my own background—he could be narrow, clannish, short-tempered, stubborn to a fault. But he could also be intensely loyal and courageous. And deeply patriotic. He was one of us, Americans said, just as they also said, "To err is Truman."

He was back in the news again after the Republican sweep in November 1994, the first such Republican triumph since 1946, and so naturally comparisons were drawn. Like Bill Clinton, Truman had been humiliated in his midterm election of 1946, treated with open scorn and belittlement by Republicans, and seldom defended by his fellow Democrats. He was written off.

But how Truman responded is extremely interesting and bears directly on our subject, character in the presidency. It was as if he had been liberated from the shadow of Roosevelt. "I'm doing as I damn please for the next two years and to hell with all of them," he told his wife, Bess. And what's so remarkable and fascinating is that the next two years were the best of Truman's presidency. The years 1947 and 1948 contained most of the landmark achievements of his time in office: the first civil rights message ever sent to Congress, his executive order to end segregation in the armed forces, the Truman Doctrine, the recognition of Israel, the Berlin Airlift, and the Marshall Plan, which saved Western Europe from economic and political ruin and stands today as one of the great American achievements of the century.

He showed again and again that he understood the office, how the government works, and that he understood himself. He knew who he was, he liked who he was. He liked Harry Truman. He enjoyed being Harry Truman. He was grounded, as is said. He stressed, "I tried never to forget who I was, where I came from, and where I would go back to."

And again and again, as I hope I will be able to demonstrate, he could reach down inside himself and come up with something very good and strong. He is the seemingly ordinary American who, when put to the test, rises to the occasion and does the extraordinary.

Now, by saying he knew himself and understood himself and liked himself, I don't mean vanity or conceit. I'm talking about self-respect, self-understanding. To an exceptional degree, power never went to his head, nor did he ever grow cynical, for all the time he spent in Washington. He was never inclined to irony or to grappling with abstract thoughts. He read a great deal, enjoyed good bourbon—Wild Turkey preferably—he was a good listener. His physical, mental, and emotional stamina were phenomenal. There's much to be seen about people in how they stand, how they walk. Look at the photographs of Harry Truman, the newsreels—backbone American.

In the spring of 1945, the new untested president of the United States sat in the Oval Office. Across the desk, in the visitor's chair, sat a grim-looking old friend, Sam Rayburn, the Speaker of the House. They were alone in the room, just the two of them, and they were, in many ways, two of a kind. Rayburn knew he could talk straight from the shoulder to Truman, who had been in office only a few days.

"You have got many great hazards and one of them is in this White House. I've been watching this thing a long time," Rayburn began. "I've seen people in the White House try to build a fence around the White House and keep the very people away from the president that he should see. That is one of your hazards, the special interests and the sycophants who will stand in the rain a week to see you and will treat you like a king. They'll come sliding in and tell you you're the greatest man alive. But you know, and I know, you ain't."

Truman knew he wasn't Hercules, he knew he wasn't a glamour boy, he knew he didn't have—and this is so important—the capacity to move the country with words, with eloquence. He had none of the inspirational magic of his predecessor. If Roosevelt was Prospero, Truman was Horatio.

Character Above All is the title of this book, and character counts in the presidency more than any other single quality. It is more important than how much the president knows of foreign policy or economics, or even about politics. When the chips are down—and the chips are nearly always down in the presidency—how do you decide? Which way do you go? What kind of courage is called upon? Talking of his hero Andrew Jackson, Truman once said, it takes one kind of courage to face a duelist, but it's nothing like the courage it takes to tell a friend no.

In making his decision to recognize Israel, Truman had to tell the man he admired above all others no—but more on that shortly.

TRUMAN HAD SEEN A lot of life long before he came to Washington. He was born in 1884. He was a full-grown, mature, nearly middle-aged man by the time of the Great War, as his generation called World War I, which was the real dividing line between the nineteenth and the twentieth centuries and the turning point in his life. Everything changed in the period after World War I, which in retrospect may be seen as the first, hideous installment of a two-part world catastrophe. Even the same characters—Hitler, Churchill, Roosevelt, Truman, MacArthur, Marshall—reappear in World War II. Growing up in Victorian Middle America, Truman came to maturity with much of the outlook, good and bad, of that very different time.

At heart he remained a nineteenth-century man. He never liked air-conditioning, hated talking by telephone. (And thank goodness, for he wrote letters instead, thousands as time went on, and as a result it is possible to get inside his life, to know what he thought and felt, in a way rarely possible with public figures, and presidents in particular.) He disliked daylight saving time and time zones. (He liked wearing two watches, one set on Eastern Standard Time, the other on Missouri time, "real time," as he called it.)

He was also a farmer, a real farmer let it be remembered, not a photo opportunity or a gentleman farmer like FDR or Tom Dewey. With his father, he *worked* on the farm, facing all the perils of bad weather, failing crops, insect plagues, and debt. Truman & Son, of Grandview, Missouri, were never out of debt. He was there for eleven years, until he went off to war in 1917, and as he used to say, "It takes a lot of pride to run a farm." Certainly on a family farm, you don't "do your own thing." Let down your end and the whole enterprise may fall. And every morning there's your father at the foot of the stairs at five-thirty, no matter the weather, no matter the season, telling you it's time to be up and at it.

There was no running water on the Truman farm, no electricity. When his mother had to have an emergency appendectomy, she was operated on by a country doctor on the kitchen table, and it was young Harry who stood beside her through all of it holding the lantern.

He was, as his pal Harry Vaughan, once said, "one tough son-of-a-bitch of a man.... And that," said Vaughan, "was part of the secret of understanding him." He could take it. He had been through so much. There's an old line, "Courage is having done it before."

It's been often said that Truman was poorly prepared for the presidency. He came to office not knowing any of the foreign policy establishment in Washington. He had no friends on Wall Street, no powerful financial backers, no intellectual "brain trust." When Winston Churchill came to Washington in the early 1940s and busied himself meeting everybody of known influence, no one suggested he look up the junior senator from Missouri.

But Truman had experienced as wide a range of American life as had any president, and in that sense, he was well prepared. He had grown up in a small town when the small town was the essence of American life. He'd been on the farm all those years, and he'd gone to war. And the war was the crucible. Captain Harry Truman returned from France in 1919 having led an artillery battery through the horrific Battle of the Argonne and having discovered two vitally important things about himself. First, that he had courage, plain physical courage. Until then he had never been in a fight in his life. He was the little boy forbidden by his mother to play in roughhouse games because of his glasses. He was a bookworm—a sissy, as he said himself later on, using the dreaded word. But in France he'd found he could more than hold his own in the face of the horrors of battle and, second, that he was good at leading people. He liked it and he had learned that courage is contagious. If the leader shows courage, others get the idea.

Often he was scared to death. One of the most endearing of his many letters to Bess was written after his first time under fire in France, to tell her how terrified he was. It happened at night in the rain in the Vosges Mountains. The Germans had opened fire with a withering artillery barrage. Truman and his green troops thought it could be the start of a gas attack and rushed about trying frantically not only to get their own gas masks on, but to get masks on the horses as well. And then they panicked, ran. Truman, thrown by his horse, had been nearly crushed when the horse fell on him. Out from under, seeing the others all running, he just stood there, locked in place, and called them back using every form of profanity he'd ever heard. And back they came. This was no Douglas MacArthur strutting the edge of a trench to inspire the troops. This was a man who carried extra eyeglasses in every pocket because without glasses he was nearly blind. He had memorized the eye chart in order to get into the army. And there he was in the sudden hell of artillery shells exploding all around, shouting, shaming his men back to do what they were supposed to do.

Now flash forward to a night thirty years later, in 1948, at the Democratic National Convention in Philadelphia, when Democrats on the left and Democrats on the right had been doing everything possible to get rid of President Harry Truman for another candidate. The Dixiecrats had marched out of the convention. The liberals, who had tried to draft General Eisenhower, were down in the dumps as never before, convinced, after Truman was nominated, that all was lost. Truman was kept waiting backstage hour after hour. It was not until nearly two in the morning that he came onstage to accept the nomination. That was the year when the conventions were covered by television for the first time, and the huge lights made even worse the summer furnace of Philadelphia. The crowd was drenched in perspiration, exhausted. For all the speeches there had been, nobody had said a word about winning.

Truman, in a white linen suit, walked out into the floodlights and did just what he did in the Vosges Mountains. He gave them hell. He told them, in effect, to soldier up—and that they were going to win. It was astounding. He brought the whole hall to its feet. He brought them up cheering. Old-hand reporters, even the most diehard liberals who had so little hope for him, agreed it was one of the greatest moments they had ever witnessed in American politics.

So there we have it, courage, determination, call it as you will. Dean Acheson, his secretary of state, much later, searching for a way to describe the effect Truman could have on those around him, and why they felt as they did about him, quoted the lines from Shakespeare's *Henry V*, when King Henry—King Harry—walks among the terrified, dispirited troops the night before the Battle of Agincourt:

> *. . . every wretch, pining and pale before,*
> *Beholding him, plucks comfort from his looks. . . .*
> *His liberal eye doth give to every one . . .*
> *A little touch of Harry in the night.*

Acheson was remembering one of the darkest times of the Truman years, when unexpectedly 260,000 Chinese Communist troops came storming into the Korean War. Through it all, as Acheson and others saw at close hand, Truman never lost confidence, never lost his essential good cheer, never lost his fundamental civility and decency toward those who worked with him. He was never known to dress down a subordinate. "Give 'em hell, Harry" never gave anybody hell behind the scenes, on the job.

His decision to go into Korea in June 1950 was the most difficult of his presidency, he said. And he felt it was the most important decision of his presidency—more difficult and important than the decision to use the atomic bomb, because he feared he might be taking the country into another still more horrible world war, a nuclear war. Yet at the time, it was a very popular decision, a point often forgotten. The country was waiting for the president to say we would go to the rescue of the South Koreans, who were being overrun by the Communist North Korean blitzkrieg. The lesson of Munich weighed heavily on everyone. In Congress, the president had strong support on both sides of the aisle, at the start at least. He was applauded by the press across the country. It was only later that summer of 1950 when the war went so sour that it became "Truman's War."

But you see, there was no corollary between popularity and the ease or difficulty of the decision. His most popular decision was, for him, his most difficult decision, while his least popular decision was, he said, not difficult at all. That was the firing of General Douglas MacArthur, by far the most unpopular, controversial act of his presidency. Attacked by all sides, torn to shreds in editorials and by radio commentators, a potent force then as today, Truman went on with his work as usual, just riding it out. He seemed to have a sort of inner gyroscope for such times. Those around him wondered how it was possible. He said he was sure that in the long run the country would judge him to have done the right thing. Besides, he had only done his duty. The Constitution stated clearly that there will be civilian control over the military and he had taken an oath to uphold the Constitution. "It wasn't difficult for me at all," he insisted.

TRUMAN'S PROFOUND SENSE OF history was an important part of his makeup. He believed every president should know American history at the least, and world history, ideally. A president with a sense of history is less prone to hubris. He knows he is but one link in a long chain going all the way back to the first president and that presumably will extend far into the future. He knows he has only a limited time in office and that history will be the final judge of his performance. What he does must stand the test of time. If he is blasted by the press, if his polls are plummeting as Truman's did during the Korean War, these are not the first concerns. What matters—or ought to matter—is what's best for the country and the world in the long run.

Truman probably understood the history of the presidency as well as or better than any president of this century with the exception of

Woodrow Wilson, and in his first years in the White House, he felt acutely the presence of his predecessors. He was sure the White House was haunted. This was before restoration of the old place, when it creaked and groaned at night with the change of temperature. Sometimes doors would fly open on their own. Alone at night, his family back in Missouri, he would walk the upstairs halls, poke about in closets, wind the clocks. He imagined his predecessors arguing over how this fellow Truman was doing so far.

His reputation seems to grow and will, I believe, continue to grow for the reason that he not only faced difficult decisions and faced them squarely, if not always correctly, but that the decisions were so often unprecedented. There were no prior examples to go by. In his first months in office, he made more difficult and far-reaching decisions than any president in our history, including Franklin Roosevelt and Abraham Lincoln. This much belittled, supposed backwater political hack, who seemed to have none or certainly very few of the requisite qualities for high office, turned out to do an extremely good job. And it is quite mistaken to imagine that nobody saw this at the time. Many did, and the closer they were to him, the more clearly they saw. Churchill, Marshall, and especially, I would say, Acheson, who was about as different from Harry Truman in background and manner as anyone could be. Acheson once remarked that he had great respect for Franklin Roosevelt, but that he reserved his love for another president, meaning Harry Truman. Acheson didn't much like Roosevelt, I suspect, because Roosevelt was condescending toward him. I imagine that if Acheson were to tolerate condescension, it would have to be Acheson being condescending toward someone else.

In the course of more than one hundred interviews for my biography of Truman, I found no one who had worked with him, no one who was on the White House staff, or the White House domestic staff, or his Secret Service detail, who did not like him. He knew everybody by name on the White House staff and in the mansion itself. He knew all the Secret Service people by name. He knew all about their families—and this wasn't just a politician's trick. If he could have picked his own father, one former Secret Service man told me, it would have been Truman.

John Gunther, in a wonderful interview with Truman when Truman was vice president, asked him what he was most interested in. "People," Truman said without hesitation.

He had a further quality, also greatly needed in the presidency: a healthy, resilient sense of humor. He loved especially the intrinsic humor of politics, the good stories of politics. Campaigning in Texas by train in 1948, he had nothing but blue skies and huge, warm crowds everywhere he stopped. The reason now was his civil rights program, which was anything but popular in Texas. There had been warnings even of serious trouble if ever he were to show his face in Texas. But his reception was good-natured and approving the whole way across the state, and Truman loved every moment. It was probably his happiest time of the whole 1948 whistle-stop odyssey. On board the train were Sam Rayburn and young Lyndon Johnson, who was running for the Senate, as well as Governor Beauford Jester, who had earlier called Truman's civil rights program a stab in the back.

But all that was forgotten in the warmth of the days and the warmth of the crowds, and at the last stop, Rayburn's hometown of Bonham, Rayburn invited the president to come by his little house on the highway, outside of town. When the motorcade arrived, hundreds of people were on the front lawn. Rayburn told them to form a line, and he would see they met the president. The Secret Service immediately objected, saying they had no identifications for anyone. Rayburn was furious. He knew every man, woman, and child on that lawn, he said, and could vouch for each and every one. So the line started for the house where Governor Jester offered greetings at the door and the president, a surreptitious bourbon within reach, shook hands with "the customers," as he called them. All was going well until Rayburn, who never took his eye off the line, shouted, "Shut the door, Beauford, they're coming through twice."

Yet for all that it is mistaken to picture Harry Truman as just a down-home politician of the old stamp. The Harry Truman of Merle Miller's

Plain Speaking, or of the play *Give 'Em Hell, Harry*, is entertaining and picturesque, but that wasn't the man who was president of the United States. He wasn't just some kind of comic hick.

Now, he did make mistakes. He was not without flaw. He could be intemperate, profane, touchy, too quick with simplistic answers. In private conversation, he could use racial and religious slurs, old habits of the mouth. In many ways his part of Missouri was more like the Old South than the Middle West, and he grew up among people who in so-called polite society commonly used such words.

Yet here is the man who initiated the first civil rights message ever and ordered the armed services desegregated. And let's remember, that was in 1948, long before Martin Luther King Jr., or *Brown v. Board of Education*, the landmark Supreme Court decision on the desegregation of schools, or the civil rights movement. When friends and advisers warned him that he was certain to lose the election in 1948 if he persisted with his civil rights program, he said if he lost for that, it would be for a good cause. Principle mattered more than his own political hide. His courage was the courage of his convictions.

Truman's greatest single mistake was the loyalty oath program, requiring a so-called loyalty check of every federal employee. It was uncalled-for, expensive, it contributed substantially to the mounting bureaucracy of Washington and damaged the reputations and lives of numbers of people who should never have had any such thing happen to them. He did it on the advice that it was good politics. He let his better nature be overcome by that argument. It was thought such a move could head off the rising right-wing cry of communists in government, the McCarthy craze then in its early stages. But it didn't work. It was shameful.

His Supreme Court appointments weren't particularly distinguished. His seizure of the steel industry during the Korean War to avert a nationwide strike was high-handed and rightly judged unconstitutional, though his motives were understandable. We were at war, and a prolonged shutdown of production of steel threatened the very lives of our fighting forces in Korea.

He himself thought one of his worst mistakes was to have allowed the pell-mell demobilization that followed World War II. Almost overnight American military might had all but vanished. When we intervened in Korea, we had little to fight with, except for the atomic bomb. That Truman refused to use the atomic bomb in Korea, despite tremendous pressure from General MacArthur and others, stands as one of his most important decisions and one for which he has been given little credit.

The idea that Harry Truman made the decision to use the bomb against Japan and then went upstairs and went to sleep is an unfortunate myth for which he is largely accountable. I think he gave that impression because he came from a time and place in America where you were not supposed to talk about your troubles. "How are you?" "I'm fine." You might be dying of some terrible disease—"I'm fine. And you?" He refused ever to talk of the weight of the decision except to say that he made it and that it was his responsibility.

He dropped the atomic bomb on Japan to end the war. Was it right? Was it wrong? I think he saw it as necessary. It is so very important to understand the atmosphere of the moment, the atmosphere in which the decision was made. We were at war. Moreover, we were suffering increasingly heavier casualties the closer we came to Japan. In Europe we had just endured horrendous losses at the hands of the supposedly defeated German Army. There were eighty thousand American casualties at the Battle of the Bulge, one of the most costly battles ever fought by Americans. Then came the bloodbath of Okinawa, with a toll greater than anyone in Washington had foreseen, some forty-nine thousand American casualties before it was over, and the Japanese were certain to fight with still greater ferocity when we invaded the home islands.

It must also be understood that by then we were sending massive, devastating B-29 raids against Japan on a routine basis. The slaughter was extreme—twenty thousand, forty thousand lives at a blow. The raid on Tokyo on March 10, 1945, may have taken one hundred thousand lives.

When Robert Oppenheimer, director of the project that developed the bomb, was asked how many casualties might result from use of the bomb, presuming it worked, he said perhaps as many as twenty thousand. Now suppose you are the president and you know these horrible raids you are sending against Japan are killing as much as twice or three times that number, and that possibly one bomb delivered by one plane might, if it worked, have the effect of shocking the enemy into surrendering and all the slaughter could stop. An invasion of Japan would become unnecessary. Thousands of American lives would be saved. And imagine also that no one among your top advisers is telling you not to use the bomb.

The president—the commander in chief—gave the order. The war ended.

WITH THE RETURN OF peace, Truman's political troubles began. The year 1946 was particularly rough. He seemed hopelessly ineffectual. He seemed to be trying to please everybody at once, willing to say to almost anybody whatever they most wanted to hear. He wasn't at all like the Harry Truman I've been describing. He had never wanted the job and for some time appeared willing to give it up as soon as possible. He tried twice to get General Eisenhower to agree to run as a Democrat in the next election, saying he would gladly step aside. According to one account, he even offered to run as vice president with Ike at the head of the ticket. But then after the setback in the '46 congressional elections, he became a different man.

Fire in the belly for presidential glory was never part of his nature. He wasn't in the job to enlarge his estimate of himself. He didn't need that. He didn't need the limelight or fawning people around him in order to feel good about being Harry Truman.

On that note, it is interesting to see whom he did choose to have around him, as a measure of his character. There were Omar Bradley and Matthew Ridgway at the Pentagon, Eisenhower at the head of NATO. George C. Marshall served as secretary of state and later as secretary of defense. There were Dean Acheson, Averell Harriman, Robert Lovett, George Kennan, Chip Bohlen, David Lilienthal, James

Forrestal, Sam Rosenman, Clark Clifford—the list is long and very impressive. That most of them had more distinguished backgrounds than he, if they were taller, handsomer, it seemed to bother him not at all. When it was suggested to him that General Marshall as secretary of state might lead people to think Marshall would make a better president, Truman's response was that, yes, of course, Marshall would make a better president, but that he, Harry Truman, was president and he wanted the best people possible around him.

As no president since Theodore Roosevelt, Truman had a way of saying things that was so much his own, and I would like to quote some of them:

"I wonder how far Moses would have gone, if he had taken a poll in Egypt."

"God doesn't give a damn about pomp and circumstance."

"There are more prima donnas in Washington than in all the opera companies."

He is also frequently quoted as having said, "If you want a friend in Washington, buy a dog," and "If you want to live like a Republican, vote Democratic." I doubt he said the first, but the second does sound like him.

"The object and its accomplishment is my philosophy," he said. Let me say that again. "The object and its accomplishment is my philosophy." And no president ever worked harder in office. At times, a little discouraged, he would say, "All the president is is a glorified public relations man who spends his time flattering, kissing and kicking people to get them to do what they are supposed to do anyway."

WHERE WERE HIS STRENGTHS and his weaknesses in conflict? In interviews with those who knew him, I would ask what they believed to have been the president's major flaw. Almost always they would say he was too loyal to too many people to whom he should not have been so loyal—not as president. They were thinking mainly of the cronies—

people like Harry Vaughan. Or remembering when Boss Tom Pendergast died, and Vice President Harry Truman commandeered an air force bomber and flew to Kansas City for the funeral. "You don't forget a friend" was Truman's answer to the press.

Tom Pendergast had made Truman, and the Pendergast machine, though colorful and not without redeeming virtues, was pretty unsavory altogether.

But Truman was also, let us understand, the product of the smoke-filled room in more than just the Kansas City way. He was picked at the 1944 Democratic Convention in Chicago in a room at the Blackstone Hotel thick with smoke. He was tapped as Roosevelt's running mate and almost certain successor by the party's big-city bosses, the professional pols, who didn't want Henry Wallace, then the vice president, because Wallace was too left wing, and didn't want Jimmy Byrnes, another Roosevelt favorite, because Byrnes was too conservative, an avowed segregationist and a lapsed Roman Catholic. They wanted Harry Truman, so Truman it was. They knew their man. They knew what stuff he was made of. And remember, this was all in a tradition of long standing. Theodore Roosevelt had been picked by a Republican machine in New York, Woodrow Wilson by the Democratic machine in New Jersey. For Franklin Roosevelt, such "good friends" as Ed Kelly of Chicago, Boss Crump of Memphis, Ed Flynn of the Bronx were indispensable. And because a candidate had the endorsement of a machine, or as in Truman's case owed his rise in politics to a corrupt organization, it didn't necessarily follow that he himself was corrupt. John Hersey, who did one of the best of all pieces ever written about Harry Truman, for *The New Yorker*, said he found no trace of corruption in Truman's record. Nor did I. Nor did the FBI when it combed through Truman's past at the time Pendergast was convicted for an insurance fraud and sent to prison. Nor did all the Republicans who ran against him in all the elections in his long political career.

I think he was almost honest to a fault. Still he understood, and felt acutely, the bargain he made with loyalty to the likes of Pendergast, and he understood why he was so often taken to task by the Republicans or the press or just ordinary citizens who didn't care for the kind of political company he kept.

Harry Vaughan was for comic relief, Truman's Falstaff. Among the delights of Truman as a biographical subject is that he enjoyed both Vaughan and Mozart. He loved a night of poker with "the boys," and he loved the National Symphony, which he attended as often as possible. If the program included Mozart or Chopin, he would frequently take the score with him.

This same Harry Truman, who adored classical music, who read Shakespeare and Cicero and *Don Quixote*, comes out of a political background about as steamy and raw as they get. And at times, this would get to him, and he would escape to the privacy of a downtown Kansas City hotel room. There he would pour himself out on paper, the innermost anguish in long memoranda to himself, and these amazing documents survive in the files of the Truman Library in Independence, Missouri, along with thousands of his letters and private diaries.

Here is a striking example written when Truman was a county judge (a county commissioner, really) and one of his fellow commissioners had made off with ten thousand dollars from the county till:

> This sweet associate of mine, my friend, who was supposed to back me, had already made a deal with a former crooked contractor, a friend of the Boss's . . . I had to compromise in order to get the voted road system carried out . . . I had to let a former saloonkeeper and murderer, a friend of the Boss's, steal about $10,000 from the general revenues of the county to satisfy my ideal associate and keep the crooks from getting a million or more out of the bond issue.

He is not exaggerating with the million-dollar figure. When the Pendergast organization collapsed and its ways of operation were revealed, a million dollars was found to be about standard. But then, importantly, Truman goes on:

Was I right or did I compound a felony? I don't know. . . . Anyway I've got the $6,500,000 worth of roads on the ground and at a figure that makes the crooks tear their hair. The hospital is up at less cost than any similar institution in spite of my drunken brother-in-law [Fred Wallace], whom I'd had to employ on the job to keep peace in the family. I've had to run the hospital job myself and pay him for it. . . . Am I an administrator or not? Or am I just a crook to compromise in order to get the job done? You judge it, I can't.

This is all very painful for him. He writes of being raised at his mother's knee to believe in honor, ethics, and "right living." Not only is he disgusted by the immorality he sees behind the scenes, he doesn't understand it.

But let me return to 1948, where I think we see Truman, the president, at his best. Consider first the crisis over Berlin. That spring the Russians had suddenly clamped a blockade around the city, which was then under Allied control though within the Russian zone of East Germany. Overnight, without warning, Berlin was cut off. Other than by air, there was no way to supply it. Two and a half million people were going to be without food, fuel, medical supplies. Clearly, Stalin was attempting to drive the Allies out. The situation was extremely dangerous.

At an emergency meeting in the Oval Office, it was proposed that the Allies break through with an armored convoy. It looked as though World War III might be about to start. It was suggested that Berlin be abandoned. Nobody knew quite what to do. Truman said, "We stay in Berlin, period." He didn't know how that could be done any more than anyone else, but he said, "We stay in Berlin." Backbone

An airlift had already begun as a temporary measure. Truman ordered it stepped up to the maximum. It was said by experts, including the mayor of Berlin, that to supply the city by air would be impossible, given the size of the planes and the calculated number of landings possible per day. The whole world was on edge.

"We'll stay in Berlin," Truman said again, "come what may." The supposedly insoluble problem of the limit of plane landings per day was nicely solved: they built another airport. The airlift worked. The Russians gave up the blockade. The crisis passed.

AMONG THE MOST DIFFICULT and important concepts to convey in teaching or writing history is the simple fact that things never had to turn out as they did. Events past were never on a track. Nobody knew at the start that the Berlin Airlift would work. It was a model, I think, of presidential decision-making and of presidential character proving decisive.

All this, I should also remind you, was taking place in an election year. Yet at no time did Truman include any of his political advisers in the discussions about Berlin. Nor did he ever play on the tension of the crisis for his own benefit in the speeches he made.

With the question of whether to recognize Israel, Truman faced an equally complex situation but one greatly compounded by emotion. Of particular difficulty for him, personally and politically, was the position of his then secretary of state, George Marshall, who was gravely concerned about Middle Eastern oil supplies. If Arab anger over American support for a new Jewish state meant a cut-off of Arab oil, it would not only jeopardize the Marshall Plan and the recovery of Europe but also could prove disastrous should the Berlin crisis indeed turn to war.

Marshall was thinking as a military man, determined to hold to a policy that was in the best interest of the United States. It was by no means a matter of anti-Semitism, as was sometimes charged, or any lack of sympathy for the idea of a Jewish homeland. But the fact that Marshall was against an immediate recognition put Truman in an extremely difficult position. No American of the time counted higher in Truman's estimate than Marshall. He saw Marshall as the modern-day equivalent of George Washington or Robert E. Lee and valued his judgment more than that of anyone in the cabinet. Further, Marshall was far and away the most widely respected member of the administration, and if Truman were to decide against him and Marshall were then to resign, it would almost certainly mean defeat for Truman in November. He could lose the respect of the man he most respected and lose the presidency.

Truman did recognize Israel—immediately, within minutes—and he never doubted he was doing the right thing. His interest in the history of the Middle East was long-standing. He had been a strong supporter of a homeland for Jewish refugees from Europe from the time he had been in the Senate. But he also knew George Marshall and was sure Marshall would stand by him, as of course Marshall did.

I HAVE SPENT A sizable part of my writing life trying to understand Harry Truman and his story. I don't think we can ever know enough about him. If his loyalty was a flaw, it was his great strength also, as shown by his steadfast loyalty to Dean Acheson when Joe McCarthy came after Acheson or the unflinching support he gave David Lilienthal when Lilienthal, Truman's choice to head the Atomic Energy Commission, was accused of being a "pink," a communist. Franklin Roosevelt had not been willing to stand up for Lilienthal. Truman did. And Lilienthal was approved by the Senate.

Perhaps Truman's greatest shortcoming was his unwillingness to let us know, to let the country know then, how much more there was to him than met the eye, how much more he was than just "Give 'em hell, Harry"—that he did have this love of books, this interest in history, his affection for people, his kindness, his thoughtfulness to subordinates, the love of music, the knowledge of music, his deep and abiding love for his wife, his bedrock belief in education and learning. Though he had never gone beyond Independence High School, this was a president who enjoyed Cicero in the original Latin. We should have known that. It's good to know now, too.

A few words about the '48 campaign, which will always be part of our political lore. It's a great American metaphor, a great American story. The fellow who hasn't got a chance comes from behind and wins.

Nobody in either party, not a professional politician, not a reporter, not even his own mother-in-law, doubted that Tom Dewey would be the next president. The result of a *Newsweek* poll of fifty top political commentators nationwide who were asked to predict the outcome was Dewey 50, Truman 0.

No president had ever campaigned so hard or so far. Truman was sixty-four years old. Younger men who were with him through it all would describe the time on the train as one of the worst ordeals of their lives. The roadbed was rough, and Truman would get the train up to eighty miles an hour at night. The food was awful, the work unrelenting. One of them told me, "It's one thing to work that hard and to stay the course when you think you're going to win, but it's quite another thing when you *know* you're going to lose." The only reason they were there, they all said, was Harry Truman.

For Truman, I think, it was an act of faith—a heroic, memorable American act of faith. The poll takers, the political reporters, the pundits, all the sundry prognosticators, and professional politicians—it didn't matter what they said, what they thought. Only the people decide, Truman was reminding the country. "Here I am, here's what I stand for—here's what I'm going to do if you keep me in the job. You decide."

Was he a great president? Yes. One of the best. And a very great American. Can we ever have another Harry Truman? Yes, I would say so. Who knows, maybe somewhere in Texas she's growing up right now.

I live in Massachusetts, and this morning, on my way to the Boston airport, I drove by the original home of John Adams. It is very modest. Adams, too, was a farmer. Listen please to what he said in the year 1765, more than a decade before Philadelphia, 1776: "Liberty cannot be preserved without general knowledge among the people who have the right to that knowledge and the desire to know. But besides this, they have a right, an indisputable, unalienable, indefeasible, divine right to that most dreaded and envied kind of knowledge—I mean of the character and conduct of their rulers."

He put character first.

PART THREE

INFLUENCES

THE LOVE OF LEARNING

DMcC's time as a student at Yale was, he felt, as profound as any period in his life. He majored in English, studied painting and art, and experienced life outside of Pittsburgh for the first time. For all of his days afterward, he was grateful to Yale.

In 2006, he was asked to deliver a speech as part of the "Yale Tomorrow" fundraising campaign. As was his wont, he put great effort into the speech, a talk about three important figures in the university's early history, Ezra Stiles, John Trumbull, and Manasseh Cutler. In researching for his remarks, he became fascinated by the story of Cutler's life and the history of the Northwest Territory, subjects that eventually led him to write The Pioneers.

"One thing leads to another" was an adage he believed in strongly.

During the question-and-answer session following a talk I gave on a California campus a while ago, I was asked, "Besides Truman and John Adams, how many other presidents have you interviewed?"

Appearances notwithstanding, I never met John Adams. I did see Mr. Truman once, in Brooklyn in 1956, at a political gathering, but we didn't speak.

I can attest, however, that for all the intervening time between John Adams's day and our own, one can indeed come to know such a man and his contemporaries quite well through what they wrote, what they read, and so much that they cared about. You can learn a lot about people by what they love.

Spend five or six years with the diaries and letters of John and Abigail Adams—and the letters number in the thousands—you get to know them in many ways as well or better than you know people in your own life. So much is there. So much is said that is so often left unsaid, except in the privacy of a journal or in heartfelt correspondence.

My subject on this grand occasion is the love of learning, as personified by three others of Adams's day, three he knew and admired—three all-out, high-voltage, eighteenth-century polymaths known for their abiding interest in all manner of things. All three were born and raised in Connecticut. All were men of uncommon accomplishment. All, like Adams, were ardent patriots, and each in his way had an impact on the history of our country. And they are, all three, part of the story of Yale.

Two are comparatively well known—the first mainly in Yale circles, the second in the field of American art. The third is hardly known, which is not at all as it should be.

At a Sterling Library dinner last year, I had the good fortune to sit beside Alice Prochaska, the head university librarian. Naturally, we got talking about books. I asked whose work today she particularly likes. She mentioned the English writer Penelope Lively and recommended her novel *Moon Tiger*, which I got hold of as soon as I could. It's dazzling, and particularly because of her sense of history.

"History," she writes, "is of course crammed with people . . . who are just sitting it out. It is the front-liners who are the exception. . . ."

None of my three can ever be said to have just sat it out. Not even for a day.

THE REVEREND DR. EZRA Stiles, class of 1746, was the seventh president of Yale College, serving through the turbulent years of the Revolutionary War and on into the beginnings of the new nation.

The college, poor and small with all of 132 students, might not have survived the war years had it not been for Stiles. And in the years following, it was he who started Yale on its way to becoming a university. But then, as fully appreciated at the time, Ezra Stiles was himself a one-man university.

Eminent clergyman and educator, he was a strong, effective speaker, vigorous correspondent, and inexhaustible diarist. (His papers are among the crown jewels of the Beinecke Library.) He was a linguist, astronomer, the father of eight children, president of the Connecticut Society for the Abolition of Slavery, and a great lover of drawing up plans and maps. He knew law, history, and ecclesiastical history especially. He knew everything under the sun, it seemed. Like all scholars of that day, he was conversant in Greek and Latin, but also Hebrew and French, and kept plugging away steadily on his Arabic.

When Governor Thomas Jefferson of Virginia came to call in 1784, Stiles and he plunged at once into a conversation about electricity, then moved on to paleontology, as Jefferson described the giant bones he had acquired from recent diggings by the Ohio River. "He has a thigh-bone *three feet long*—and a tooth weighing *sixteen pounds*," Stiles recorded enthusiastically.

Stiles was a tiny, fragile, birdlike man. He stood not much over five feet tall. Yet he was never less than impressive in his white wig and academic robes. Students remembered the intent look in his eyes.

You may see for yourself in one of the outstanding portraits in the permanent collection of the Yale Art Gallery. Time with this picture is well spent. How much, we wonder, had he come to know and understand that we don't. What would we give to talk with such a man.

The picture was painted by Samuel King in 1771. People who sit for their portraits often want some bit of staging, a prop or two included to show what matters to them and what they wish to be remembered for. Stiles sits, Bible in hand, amid shelves of books and an astronomical chart, and lest there be any puzzlement over the meaning of all this, he spelled it out in his diary.

"This day Mr. King finished my picture," he began, then proceeded to name every book on the shelves—the volumes of Roman and Chinese history, the Talmud, Newton's *Principia*, Plato. "The Newtonian and Pythagorean system of sun and planets," as diagrammed to the left of his head, are, he tells us, "emblems . . . more descriptive of my mind than the effigy of my face."

Stiles dearly loved show and ceremony and saw that much was made of academic rituals and Yale commencements. He loved conferring honorary degrees, and John Adams and Thomas Jefferson were among the first he so honored.

He was a devout and liberal Christian, and as a minister of the gospel, a strong voice for religious tolerance. An early champion of the glorious cause of America, as it was known, he remained, he said, "an unchanged Son of Liberty." He cherished time in the classroom and seemed capable of teaching everything, and very nearly did while serving as president. In the last years of his life, he was still attending classes, overseeing exams, and blazing his way through new books. In the last years of his life especially, he was widely regarded as the most learned man in America.

As Professor Edmund Morgan has written in his splendid biography, Stiles "still kept sacred his omnivorous curiosity," always "more interested in what he did not know than in what he did."

Ezra Stiles died while still in office in 1795. He was succeeded by Timothy Dwight, who is another story.

AMONG THE GREAT SIGHTS to be seen in New Haven in the late 1830s was a proud, dignified gentleman of advanced years, one of the last of the veterans of the Revolution, taking his usual walk under the elms along Hillhouse Avenue, always perfectly attired, and still handsome in his eighties.

It was old John Trumbull, the "patriot-artist," Colonel John Trumbull, who had served as an aide to General Washington (as he never let anyone forget) and who had recently bestowed on Yale a large collection of his portraits and scenes from the Revolution, close to a hundred paintings, fifty-five of which were on display in the new Trumbull Art Gallery.

Trumbull's gift to Yale, in return for an annuity of one thousand dollars a year, was one of the greatest and most important gifts ever received by any college or university. There is no comparable collection. Its value is beyond reckoning. As Helen Cooper, Yale's curator of American art, says, how can one possibly put a price tag on his *Declaration of Independence*, to name but one example.

The Trumbull Gallery, designed by Trumbull, was the first museum on any campus in the nation. It was Greek Revival in style and stood here on the Old Campus, right about where we are now.

John Trumbull was the son of Connecticut governor John Trumbull and was the youngest member of his class to graduate in 1773 from Harvard. He might have given his work to Harvard. He thought about it, he said. "I first thought of Harvard, but she was rich, and amply endowed. I then thought of Yale. . . . She was within my native state, and poor."

His best-known work is the large rendition of *The Declaration of Independence* that hangs in the Rotunda of the Capitol in Washington. It's been seen by more people than any other single painting by an American, as thousands of visitors, day after day, have gazed upon it for nearly two hundred years. But it is the much smaller version, his original *Declaration of Independence*, the one hanging here at Yale, that is the masterpiece.

A childhood accident had left Trumbull with the use of only one eye, and so, because of his limited depth perception, he was often at his best working small. Many of his finest portraits are miniatures. Beautifully detailed, jewellike in color, it's as if they were done with a jeweler's glass.

Little about Trumbull's *Declaration of Independence, 4 July 1776*, as it is titled, is historically accurate. The draperies are wrong, the chairs are wrong, the doors are in the wrong place. No such colorful, military decoration filled the back wall of the room at Independence Hall. Nor did the delegates to the Continental Congress ever convene all together as portrayed. Nor was the Declaration signed on July 4.

One thing, however, is *quite* accurate and was the result of Trumbull's own single-minded determination. The faces are right—because he spent years sketching and painting from life as many as possible of those who had signed the Declaration, traveling up and down the country at his own expense. He wanted them recorded as individuals—*identifiable, accountable*. He cared passionately that his countrymen know who they were and remember what they did.

It was not long after the Revolution, while studying with the American master Benjamin West in London, when Trumbull decided to paint the great moments and heroes of the war. The first canvas was *The Death of General Warren at the Battle of Bunker's Hill*. When Abigail Adams saw it for the first time, during a visit to West's London studio, her heart all but stopped. She had never seen a work of art that so moved her.

"He is the first painter who has undertaken to immortalize by his pencil [brush] that great action that gave birth to our nation," she wrote to her sister. "By this means he will not only secure his own fame, but transmit to posterity characters and actions which will command the admiration of future ages, and prevent the period which gave birth to them from ever passing away into the dark abyss of time."

Trumbull was then not quite thirty years old.

In a striking self-portrait, he later portrayed himself with brushes and palette, but also the hilt of his Revolutionary War sword. He wanted to be remembered as the patriot-artist *and* patriot-soldier.

In a long, exceedingly eventful life, John Trumbull was many things—soldier, artist, teacher (Yale's first teacher of the history of art), diplomat (and possibly a spy), merchant (at which he was notably unsuccessful), architect, and author. In addition to the Trumbull Gallery, he had earlier, when Ezra Stiles was still president, provided architectural drawings for a major expansion of the college—drawings to be seen on display today at the Sterling Library. His *Autobiography* was the first by an American artist. By the time he moved to New Haven, he had come to know virtually all the prominent figures of his time on both sides of the Atlantic.

In the New Haven years, Trumbull lived with his devoted nephew, the incomparable Benjamin Silliman, Yale's first professor of chemistry and natural history, in a house on Hillhouse Avenue.

It should be noted also that along with the paintings he bequeathed to Yale, Trumbull included his own mortal remains and those of his wife, Sarah. They were to be interred in the Trumbull Gallery, he stipulated, below his life portrait of Washington. Trumbull died in 1841. Twice in the time since, as larger gallery space was needed, Yale dutifully moved the remains of John and Sarah. They lie today in the basement of the Art Gallery, and, yes, below the Washington portrait.

THOUGH THE HIGH ADVENTURES and accomplishments of Dr. Manasseh Cutler are all but unknown in our day, there is plenty about him in the historical record, including his own spirited diary entries beginning in 1765, the year Cutler was graduated from Yale College, and ending the year of his death, 1823.

If the biblical name Manasseh strikes you as odd, consider that among his Yale classmates were a Hezekiah, a Radulphus, a Theophilus, and two named Guilielmus!

Even in the eighteenth century, the heyday of polymaths, Manasseh Cutler stood out. His intellectual energy and range of interests were astonishing. He was three doctors in one—doctor of divinity, doctor of law, and medical doctor—and at one time or other, he practiced all three professions. Besides, he was a storekeeper, botanist, astronomer, army chaplain during the Revolution, and a congressman for two terms. The father of eight children, he also conducted a boarding school in the large, roomy parsonage beside the Congregational Church of Ipswich, Massachusetts, where he served as pastor for the better part of a long life. Both church and house are still there.

Cutler was activity writ large and was himself writ large physically. Seen beside frail little Ezra Stiles, whom he warmly admired, he looked as though he were of another species. Tall, massive, he dressed always in ministerial black, black velvet suit, black stockings.

But don't picture a somber fellow. He loved an entertaining story, good food, good company. He could outtalk almost anyone and was seldom happier than when politicking. "Social and genial, he was a lover of good cheer," reads an old account, "a merry laugh was his delight." From numerous of his diary entries, it's also evident that he had an eye for handsome women.

Intensely serious in his love of botany, he was the first to attempt a systematic account of the flora of New England. Pages of his diary are taken up with astronomical observations. Once, carrying a barometer, he climbed to the top of Mount Washington in New Hampshire, New England's highest mountain. When I read that he miscalculated the elevation at the summit by no less than 2,600 feet, I felt that here, too, was a fellow human being.

Yet for all that Manasseh Cutler packed into one life, it was what he did in the year 1787 that mattered above all. It was the role he played in the creation of the Northwest Ordinance that we should know him for.

The Northwest Ordinance was one of the most far-reaching steps in the right direction in our whole history. It was passed by the Congress under the old Articles of Confederation in the summer of 1787 and determined the social, political, and educational institutions for a vast territory that was to include the five great states of Ohio, Indiana, Illinois, Michigan, and Wisconsin. And it forever prohibited slavery in those states—even before we had a constitution.

The Northwest Ordinance set the standards—very high standards—for a huge inland empire larger than all of France, from which would come so much that we think of as distinctly American, from Abraham Lincoln to the Wright brothers, from the rise of Chicago to Henry Ford and Frank Lloyd Wright and Oprah Winfrey and John Glenn, and a conspicuous wealth of colleges and universities.

Manasseh Cutler played a lead role in the final draft of the ordinance itself, but it was especially as its most energetic and effective lobbyist that he shined.

It is quite a story. In the early summer of 1787, he set off for New York to lobby Congress for the ordinance and negotiate a grant from the government of five million acres, more than a million of which were for the new Ohio Company, an enterprise hatched in Boston by Cutler, General Rufus Putnam, and several other Revolutionary War veterans. He recorded vividly his journey from Ipswich to New York, the people he met along the way, and all those with whom he dealt in his lobbying campaign. He was tireless, and he succeeded.

Before the year was out, the great migration west from New England was underway. It was called "Ohio Fever." On December 3, 1787, the first wagons bound for Ohio departed from in front of Manasseh Cutler's church in Ipswich, where today a roadside marker proclaims the historic moment.

Cutler stayed behind, but the following summer, no longer able to contain himself, he lit out for Ohio, traveling light and at breakneck speed in a sulky. He traveled from Ipswich to the new Ohio settlement of Marietta on the Muskingum River, a distance of 751 miles, in 29 days, or on average better than 26 miles a day, top speed then.

There was so much to be seen, so much to record—giant trees in Ohio such as he had never imagined, a white oak one hundred feet high, a black walnut forty-six feet in diameter by his measurements. There were the Indians he met. "We have had Indians to dine almost every day . . . Delawares, Wyandots . . . Shawnees, Mingo, Seneca." He studied soils, snakes, fish in the "beautiful" Ohio River. He climbed and walked among ancient Indian mounds or monuments, utterly fascinated. But then how could he not have been?

It was Cutler who insisted that ample land, the equivalent of two townships, "be given perpetually for the purpose of a university." Ohio University at Athens was established in 1805. It was the first institution of higher learning west of the Alleghenies. At the center of the campus still stands its handsome old first building appropriately named Cutler Hall.

As Cutler wrote later to a son, "It is well known to all concerned with me in transacting the business of the Ohio Company that the establishment of a university was a first objective and lay with great weight on my mind."

Cutler never went back to Ohio after his flying visit. It does not appear that he was recompensed for all his efforts or that he expected to be. But a few years later, Ezra Stiles conferred upon him an honorary degree, which doubtless pleased him as much as anything could have.

SO THERE YOU HAVE them, the college president, the patriot-painter, and the politicking pastor, three who made a difference. Think of the example they set of how much can be made of a single life. Think of the reach of their influence. Think how such spirit as they personified remains the spirit of the Yale we have been privileged to be part of in our time.

I close with one further scene particularly fitting, I think, for this gathering of September 30, 2006. It is from Manasseh Cutler's wonderful diary. On his fateful journey to New York to lobby for the Northwest Ordinance, Cutler stopped here in New Haven. It had been years since he had returned to Yale, and he wrote at some length about his visit. Here is his account of the morning of Tuesday, July 3, 1787. As you will see, he thought his beloved alma mater could stand some improvement.

> Breakfasted this morning with Dr. Stiles.... Immediately after breakfast the tutors came in to invite me to the College. Dr. Stiles accompanied us. We took a view of the Library, the Philosophy Chamber [the science lab].... The Library is small; the collection consists principally of rather antiquated authors. The Philosophical [scientific] apparatus is still less valuable—an air pump, tolerably good; a reflecting telescope, wholly useless, for the large and small

mirrors are covered with rust, occasioned by poking in greasy fingers; a microscope of the compound kind, but very ancient; a miserable electrical machine; a large homely orrery made by one of the students; a hydrostatic balance, and a few other articles not worth naming. [And now listen to this:] *A handsome sum, however, is now being collected for purchasing a complete philosophical apparatus!*

So here's to the giving and collecting of "handsome sums" for Yale! On we go.

TRIBUTE TO VINCENT SCULLY

DMcC loved school. He said that as a child and adolescent other kids would bemoan the arrival of September, but he couldn't wait for the school bells to ring. The night before the first day, he said, he would hardly be able sleep because he was so excited to get back to it.

As an adult he told stories often about his teachers from the Linden School, Shady Side, and Yale. They were people his children came to feel we knew—Miss Mavis Bridgewater, Lowell Innes, Carl Cochran, Deane Keller, Rocky Flint, and perhaps most of all, Vincent Scully. He often described "Scully" as he performed onstage: his energy, his youth, his theater. It was Scully who opened DMcC's eyes to architecture and, I think, to the magic of what could be conveyed from the stage.

In 1999, at the National Building Museum in Washington, DC, DMcC delivered an address to inaugurate the museum's Vincent Scully Prize. His professor who became his friend, Vincent Scully, was in the audience.

Rarely has the spotlight of acclaim in this our capital city fallen on a subject so deserving as it does here tonight.

And I feel particularly honored to take part in the occasion—to speak as a friend of Vincent Scully of more than forty years and as one of the thousands of his former students—all those English majors, the history and biology and electrical engineering majors—who did not become architects or art historians or architectural critics or urbanists, yet are no less grateful for all he did to enlarge our lives.

As I remember, it began with Stonehenge. Into room 100 and onto the platform came this spare, young assistant professor with the quick stride and an intense, kind face. And at once, no time wasted, with the lights down and views of Stonehenge filling a huge screen, he was underway. And so were we.

It was 1953, the fall of my junior year, and by the end of the hour, I knew that not in fourteen years as a student had I ever experienced a class to compare to it.

Like so many here tonight, Vince, I remember whole lectures you gave, so many vivid moments in those heartfelt adventures you embarked on before our eyes, those so often breathtaking performances.

But I treasure, too, the chance remarks, nothing that you would remember, but that for the young fellow listening to you were like great intakes of oxygen.

There was one spring evening when you and I were coming out of the Elizabethan Club just as the last sun of the day had set the tower of Strathcona glowing like gold.

"Look what that building does with the light," you said. "That's what architects build with after all, light."

Once, I told Professor Scully about a book I was reading, and later he told me he had bought a copy and read it, too. Never had a teacher paid me such a compliment.

There is so much that he understands, so much that he has thought about and written about with such telling insight in his marvelous books. And in the books, too, he is teaching, always teaching, and the prospects seem boundless—Greece, Rome, Vézelay, the French gardens of André Le Nôtre, *Finnegans Wake*. And America. I think Vincent Scully may understand America better than anyone because he is so much of it in himself, heart and soul, mind and spirit.

He is Yale *and* New Haven. He is Gettysburg *and* Taos. The list could be long.

A wise professor of child development once said, "We don't teach children. We just give them who we are. And they catch that. Attitudes are caught not taught. If you love something in front of a child, the child will catch that."

It fits all of us and, of course, far beyond childhood. Vincent Scully gives us who he is. He shows us what he loves, and we catch that.

But then he has the gift, too, doesn't he?

Somewhere back there among his people there was surely a lovely, brave, clear-eyed poet for whom we can all be thankful.

He makes us see, this extraordinary American of our time. He makes us think, and with the heart no less than the mind.

GETTING THROUGH TO SCHLESINGER

The title of this piece notwithstanding, the influence on DMcC that he writes about was President John F. Kennedy. Like so many young Americans, DMcC was moved by President Kennedy to contribute to his country. After the election of 1960, he left his job at Time, Inc. in New York City, moved his family to Washington, and worked for the United States Information Agency, under Edward R. Murrow. He was twenty-seven years old and the editor of a magazine about American life and culture published for readers in the Middle East.

In his files was this piece, written it seems only for himself, sometime after President Kennedy was assassinated in November 1963.

Like millions of other Americans in the fall of 1960, I found as the presidential campaign picked up momentum that I was becoming increasingly fascinated with the two candidates and increasingly concerned about the outcome. In fact, unlike most other Americans, it was not long until I became convinced that a Nixon victory would be an absolute disaster for the country. Kennedy had to win, and I, if it was at all possible, had to do something about it. What that something might be remained a mystery until one morning, while reading the paper on the train to work, I began studying what the two candidates had been saying the day before and came up with what, to me at the moment, seemed a positive brainstorm. For the next several days, I worked the idea out in my mind. I talked about it with a number of friends, all of whom said they thought I was onto something.

My next step was to get the idea to Kennedy. And here I came face-to-face with what, to me in the fall of 1960, seemed a question of enormous importance: Was it possible for one man, one voter (me) to get one simple idea to one other man, when that other man happened to be the candidate for the president of the United States? If the answer was no, then, clearly, the Republic was heading for disaster.

I knew if I wrote a letter, the chances of its reaching Kennedy would be about one in a million, if that. Odds on a telegram getting through might be better, but only slightly. I could pick up the phone and try to bluff my way through, but I didn't have the nerve for that. Nor did I know anyone close to Kennedy, or anyone who knew anyone close to Kennedy. My one hope, it seemed, was to talk to enough friends with the hope that someone might help. I was working at *Time* then, in the promotion department. If I had been on the editorial staff, there undoubtedly would have been little trouble getting through. But I wasn't, and I didn't know any of the editors well enough to ask for help. One of the people I did talk to was Mary Tweedy, who was then head of *Time*'s education department. She suggested I try going after Arthur Schlesinger. After all, she said, he is writing most of the speeches. She had read that he was in town staying at the Carlyle.

I called the Carlyle that afternoon. Schlesinger, like the Kennedy he describes in his book *A Thousand Days*, picked up his own phone. I told him who I was and that I had an idea for Senator Kennedy. I said it was not an "I will go to Korea" sort of idea. That it was nothing so grandiose. But that I thought it might help and would he see me. He said he would like to but that he was about to leave for Cambridge. I asked him if he would see me in Cambridge. (This was not quite so aggressive as it sounds. My wife had just had our third child in Boston and was still in the hospital there. I was leaving to see her the next day, Friday.)

Schlesinger said he would see me in his office in the Harvard library at two o'clock Saturday afternoon.

At two o'clock Saturday afternoon, I was at his office, but no one was about. Coming across the campus, I had passed hundreds of students and their dates all heading in the other direction, across the river to the Harvard stadium. It was the afternoon of the Harvard-Dartmouth game, a beautiful, clear New England afternoon, the sort of afternoon when every young man should be at a football game and not waiting outside the office of a busy and, I had heard, arrogant braintruster who would probably never show up anyway.

About two thirty-five he came down the hall. He invited me into his office and sat me down on a daybed that had a green spread over it and was pushed against a wall covered with books. He pulled up a heavy wooden armchair directly in front of me, sat down, and said, "Well, what's on your mind?" At which point I proceeded to unravel my idea. For weeks it had been my major preoccupation. It had seemed of momentous import in itself, and getting it across the great divide of anonymity and millions of people and all the overwhelming bigness of big-time politics had been a burning personal cause. Now, as I sat looking at him, suddenly the whole thing seemed to dissolve like sugar in a fire. As I talked, I had the awful feeling that I was making a terrible fool of myself, that Schlesinger, perched there in his chair, puffing on his cigar, staring at me, unblinking, with eyes bigger than life behind his heavy glasses, was thinking me an impertinent, time-wasting fool. But I also thought, You've come this far, see it through and to hell with it.

I suppose I talked for fifteen minutes, nonstop. I didn't want him to say anything until I was through. I was fearful if I let him get a word in, that the word might well be *scram*. My idea, which now doesn't seem all that much, was essentially this: Nixon goes whichever way he thinks the wind's blowing. He has no character and no convictions. Moreover, he is appealing to all the worst instincts in the people. His is an unctuous sermon based on fear. Don't rock the boat, don't make waves, hold her steady as she goes, or all manner of horrors will fall upon us. Kennedy, on the other hand, is saying let's get going again. He is appealing to our best instincts. His is a call for courage. And—and this was what I felt had to be said and said hard—his courage was the courage of his convictions. I said this, and more, and I said it with enthusiasm. How much sense I made, I am not sure. When I finished talking, there was a long, silent pause. Then Schlesinger took the cigar out of the center of his mouth and said, "I think you have something. Do you have it written down?" I said I did not. "Well, write it for me," he said. "What do you want?" I asked. "A speech," he said. "And write it soon."

The interview was over. The choice was clear: Put up or shut up. For the next three nights I wrote. Never did anything come so easy. The problem was turning it off. I could hear Kennedy's voice the whole time I worked. I could see the quick hand chopping at the air, the head tilted back, the light across the top of the head. It was like writing dialogue for a vital and compelling character in a play. It was great fun.

I sent the speech to Schlesinger and began waiting. Several days passed, far too many days, it seemed. Again I had that sick feeling that I was being a fool, that Schlesinger had simply gotten rid of me in the simplest way possible. Then an envelope arrived with a Cambridge return address on it. As I took it out of the mailbox, I noticed that it had the same weight and thickness as the envelope I had sent off. (He has returned it! The bastard!) I opened it up, and inside was a fresh copy of a speech and attached was a note from Schlesinger. It read, "Here goes. Let's see what, if anything, happens." That was all. The speech was my speech with a new lead and a new end and a great deal of very skillful cutting and editing in between. For the next two weeks, I read everything candidate Kennedy was saying, listened to every news broadcast, waited for the great moment. Finally, on the Saturday night before election day, in Chicago, he gave a speech in which there was one paragraph that had one sentence written by me.

This should and could have been the end of the story, but it was not. There are two further incidents worth putting down.

One goes back to that glittering time after the election. I stopped by

Mary Tweedy's office to talk about the happy days that seemed to be here again. She told me then that she had been telling a number of her friends the story of my journey to Schlesinger and that everyone was fascinated by it. A few, she said, had told her that the story had influenced their vote, that what they liked was the idea that it was possible for just anybody to get through to the Kennedys with an idea.

The last incident is that in February of 1961, in the early days of the New Frontier, I went to work for the US Information Agency, USIA. Don Wilson, who had been the *Life* bureau chief in Washington and had become deputy director of the USIA under Edward R. Murrow, asked me to come to Washington to edit one of the agency's magazines. Not quite three years later, the day after Kennedy had been murdered, Wilson asked me to help put together a special issue on Kennedy and Johnson that could be circulated overseas in several languages. I said I thought most of the issue should be by writers of stature and that getting them on such short notice and at such a time would be extremely difficult, but that we should try. My first call was to Allan Nevins in California, who agreed immediately to write a piece on the presidency. William S. White then agreed to write on Lyndon Johnson. The final question was who should write on Kennedy. Several days had passed, and we were getting close to our deadline. I told Wilson that I thought it should be a historian and that the most appropriate historian would be Schlesinger. He agreed but said he thought it would be a great imposition. Then he said that if I wanted to try, to go ahead. I called Schlesinger at his home on Thanksgiving Day. I told him who I was and why I was calling. He said he would write the piece and that I would have it by my deadline, which was the following Monday. I did and it was superb. Whether or not he ever put my name together with the young man who came up to Cambridge, I don't know.

TRIBUTE TO PAUL HORGAN

These are remarks delivered in 1985 at Washington College in Chestertown, Maryland, at an event honoring DMcC's friend and mentor, novelist, historian, and painter Paul Horgan.

The first time I visited the Wesleyan University campus in Middletown, Connecticut, four years ago, I was met by an extraordinary welcoming committee comprised of a noted biographer, an acclaimed novelist, a prize-winning historian, an accomplished painter, a music scholar, a celebrated teacher and platform speaker, a lifelong bookman—critic and collector—and a profound humanist. I have never felt myself among such distinguished company.

He introduced himself as Paul Horgan.

FOR TODAY, I HAD hoped I might find a word or expression from the world of theater, a world Paul knows so well, signifying that moment when somebody from the chorus steps forward to say or sing a few lines of his own, then steps back again. For that is my part here. I am but one of so many who have spoken in praise of the incomparable Paul Horgan.

The chorus began almost from the moment he appeared in print, and it has never stopped. Listen:

"Its virtuosity is undeniable," wrote the New York *Herald-Tribune* of *No Quarter Given*. The book, said the Philadelphia *Ledger*, "has such strength, such sweep and power and deep insight that the total result is magnificent."

Seán Ó Faoláin praised its "imaginative beauty." The London *Observer* said, "The very excellence of [Mr. Horgan's] workmanship makes one, most unfairly, hesitate to realize the magnitude of his achievement. He has all the gifts: a style whose sheer descriptive force carries it near to magnificence; a sympathetic but quite ruthless insight into the main movement and petty subterfuges of human character; the power to build up a large structure and yet maintain proportion between the parts...."

"Paul Horgan," said a Chicago reviewer, "is destined to become one of the great ones of this earth."

That was in 1935, fifty years ago.

Carl Carmer called the magnum opus *Great River*, Horgan's four-century chronicle of the Rio Grande, "one of the major masterpieces of American historical writing."

"A work of grandeur," said *The Houston Post*. "[It has] a feeling of ageless power and destiny that are akin to faith."

Of Paul Horgan the historian, *The New York Times* has said, "He is lyrical and earthy with equal ease; his pages are exquisite blendings of man's atavistic memories and his eternal gropings toward a higher plane."

A Distant Trumpet, published in 1960, the novel that brought Paul his largest audience, was acclaimed by *The New York Times*, as "the finest novel yet of the southwest." Other papers called it "the most distinguished novel of the year" ... "thrilling" ... "a major novel, in every way exceptional" ... "a monumental work by a monumental writer."

A St. Louis review of the novel *The Thin Mountain Air* said, "Paul Horgan is one of a handful of writers in America today who deserve the title of literary master."

He has been compared to Tolstoy, Henry James, and Thomas Hardy. Historians rank him with William H. Prescott and Francis Parkman. He is the writer's writer, the biographer's biographer. Leon Edel calls his *Lamy of Santa Fe* "one of the great American biographies of all times." Novelist Walker Percy says, "No writer around has more honorable credentials," and calls the Horgan novel *Things as They Are* "a lovely, lovely job . . . a truly remarkable book." And Wallace Stegner: "I am aware," writes Stegner, "in story after story [of Horgan's] . . . not only of a sensibility, but of a serene, large, understanding mind."

Of America East & West is the Horgan anthology published just last year. It was acclaimed a "monument to moral sensibility" by *The Christian Science Monitor*. Paul Horgan, said *The Boston Globe*, is "a valuable man."

He is, he is.

OR LET US CONSIDER the man by the company he keeps. Over the years, east and west, he has counted among his close friends all of the following:

The painter Peter Hurd and Henriette Wyeth . . . her brother Andrew Wyeth and the indomitable N. C. Wyeth, founder of the Chadds Ford dynasty . . . the Fergusson family of New Mexico—Harvey and Erna Fergusson, brother and sister, were both accomplished writers and historians . . . Frank Capra, Senator Clinton Anderson, and J. Robert Oppenheimer, who, like Peter Hurd, was a friend from boyhood . . . Henry Steele Commager, Senator Daniel Patrick Moynihan, Father Theodore Hesburgh, Douglas Cater . . . C. P. Snow, Vera Zorina, Edmund Wilson, and Igor Stravinsky.

And what a gift of friendship he has given *them*.

"His devotion is so warm and dazzling and profound," Henriette Wyeth Hurd told me over the phone yesterday. "I have never felt that either my husband or I ever quite measured up to all that Paul thought we were.

"He is always giving," she said. "Most people don't, you know. People can be so pinched and cold. Paul is always giving."

Of Stravinsky, Paul has written: "His capacity for life always reached ahead." Which could be said of the Hurds also or most all the others I've named and, of course, especially of Paul himself.

PAUL IS EIGHTY-ONE. BUT as he once said of Stravinsky, his age is the least relevant detail about him.

He was born in Buffalo, New York, August 1, 1903, the second of three children in a close-knit family of comfortable means, strong Catholic faith, and extraordinary creative vitality.

"Everybody around me was talented and gave everybody talent," he once told me. "Everybody painted. My mother had a beautiful voice. My father was a marvelous drawing-room actor."

The Horgan side was Irish. His adored father, Edward Daniel Horgan—the sovereign father, as he says—was vice president of a profitable printing business owned by Paul's maternal grandfather, a stately old German with a silver-headed walking stick and the memorable name of Matthias Rohr. You can find him in *Things as They Are*, where he is called Grosspa, as you can also find Paul's father and the mother with the beautiful voice, Rose Marie Rohr Horgan.

He was christened Paul George Vincent O'Shaughnessy Horgan. And as time went on, he was judged so versatile by family and friends that they thought he might never amount to anything.

His first published book was *The Fault of Angels*, a novel. It appeared in 1933, the year Hitler and Franklin Roosevelt came to power. In the time since, he has published more than forty books, including sixteen more novels, four volumes of short stories, five works of biography, one major history in two volumes, two juveniles, and a collection of notes and reflections on writing—all this, as he says, built on an apprenticeship of five earlier novels, which he discarded.

He has won two Pulitzer Prizes, one in history for his two-volume epic *Great River* in 1955, another in biography for his *Lamy of Santa Fe* in 1975.

He has lectured at Yale, the University of Iowa, and Wesleyan, where for five years he also headed the Center for Advanced Studies.

He has been a Guggenheim Fellow, an honorary trustee of the Aspen Institute of Humanistic Studies, chairman of the board of the Santa Fe Opera, a fellow of the Morgan Library. All told, if I have counted correctly, he has twenty honorary doctoral degrees—quite apart from the fact that he never went to college.

IN 1915, WHEN PAUL was twelve, his father, who had contracted tuberculosis, pulled up stakes in Buffalo and moved the family west to the high, dry climate and open spaces of New Mexico. Eight years later, two years after his father's death, twenty-year-old Paul Horgan came east again, to Rochester, New York, and the Eastman School of Music—resolved to be an artist of one kind or another, but whether as a painter, poet, singer, or writer, he wasn't sure. And he had reason to be puzzled: He could sing, paint, act, and write.

For the time being he settled on singing instructions, but ultimately he chose to be a writer, because only as a writer could he make use of all four talents. A writer must see with the painter's eye; a writer must have an ear for the music of words; a writer must have the actor's gift for mimicry, the capacity to take any part.

"I am everyone in my novel," he explains. "If this were not so, no one in my novel would have a chance to ring true, even as I work to make each character an individual, different from the rest."

Recalling the young Paul Horgan who came to stay so often with the Wyeths at Chadds Ford, Henriette Hurd says, "He could become Louis XIV in an instant. Or put on a hat and be Napoleon or Washington, depending on how he pinched the hat."

The singing instructions ended after a year, but for two more years he stayed on in Rochester as a set designer and production assistant for the Eastman Theater under Rouben Mamoulian. Rouben Mamoulian and N. C. Wyeth, he tells me, were the two men who had the greatest influence on him in that formative time of his life.

In 1926 he went back to New Mexico and began to write, supporting himself with a position as librarian at the New Mexico Military Institute in Roswell, a school he had attended following his father's death. Except for the years of the Second World War, when he served in the army, in the Technical Information Branch in Washington, New Mexico remained his home until 1962, when he moved to Connecticut.

The east–west sides of his life, the play of east and west through his work, may seem divisive. At least one close student of his work sees exile in the West as a major Horgan theme. But I see Horgan's east and west as a span, a creative arc. Over and over in the novels and histories and biographies, his central characters are people who go far, literally and figuratively. But to appreciate how far, it is essential that we know from where they began. So origins are always important in Horgan's view of life.

Lamy's beginnings in France are as vital to our appreciation of the full man as are the empty landscapes and crystal skies of frontier New Mexico. And here, of course, the creative arc is not merely continental in scale. East isn't just Rochester, New York, but France.

Or there is this about the origins of the Spanish who ventured here. It is one of my favorite passages in *Great River*:

> They believed that, with the love of God, nothing failed; without it, nothing prospered. . . . Thus seeking their love across mountain and strand, neither gathering flowers nor fearing beasts, they would pass fortress and frontier, able to endure all because of their strength of spirit in companionship of their Divine Lord.
>
> Such belief existed within the Spanish not as a compartment where they kept their worship and faith, but as a condition of their very being, like the touch by which they felt the solid world, and the breath of life they drew until they died. It was the simplest and yet the most significant fact about them, and more than any other accounted

for their achievement in the new world. With mankind's imperfect material—for they knew all their failings, indeed, reveled in them and beat themselves with them and knew death was too good for them if Christ had to suffer so much thorn and lance and nail for them—they yet could strive to fulfill the divine will, made plain to them by the Church. Belief from man's faulty nature could be had only in God. In obedience to Him, they found their greatest freedom, the essential freedom of the personality, the individual spirit in the self, with all its other expressions which they knew well—irony, extravagance, romance, vividness and poetry in speech, and honor, and hard pride.

That also, you see, is American east and west. And the man, you see, can write like an angel.

Courage is a prevailing theme—but courage derived from faith or from experience—like the little boy in *Things as They Are* who is afraid of the lightning. Courage combined with intelligence is best of all, Horgan is telling us repeatedly.

He never forgets the human stakes in a situation. He is fascinated by communities of all kinds and by "man's ways of constantly reshaping himself as a social being."

He prizes independence. There is the bugler in *A Distant Trumpet*, young Olin Rainey, breaking away from his narrow house and alcoholic father to a life of uncertain freedom and adventure. Or Igor Stravinsky, who must remain independent of casual friendships.

Through nearly all he writes, there is a continuing fascination with light. Horgan works with light—with his "painter's eye." We encounter "bright drops of light" . . . "beads of light" . . . "golden afternoon sunlight" . . . "the delicate restrained light of Sunday afternoon" . . . "furious sunlight" . . . "pure sunlight" . . . lamplight in windows, lamplight spilling in warm pools over tables and chairs.

He is brilliant at portraiture, this painter with his eye for detail. Listen to his description of King Charles of Spain, another of my favorite passages from *Great River*:

King Charles, who was also the Holy Roman Emperor, lived and worked in hard bare rooms with no carpets, crowding to the fire in winter, using the window's sunshine in summer. The doctors of medicine stated that the humors of moisture and of cold dominated his quality. His face was fixed in calm, but for his eyes, which moved and spoke more than his gestures or his lips. His face was pale and long, the lower lip full and forward, often dry and cracked so that he kept on it a green leaf to suck. His nose was flat, and his brows were pitted with a raised frown that appeared to suggest a constant headache. He held his shoulders high as though on guard. He would seem to speak twice, once within and fully, and then outwardly and meagerly. But his eyes showed his mind, brilliant, deep, and always at work. He loved information for its own sake, was always reading, and knew his maps well. They said he saw the Indies better than many who went there and held positive views on all matters concerning the New World and its conquerors.

His writing has ranged across four hundred years of history. He writes of opera, theater, music, art, politics, military matters, the natural sciences, church history, intellectual history—and much that is futile or cruel or tragic in life.

I think of the dead two-year-old child in the coffin on the backseat of the car in the story called "The Peach Stone" or the touching child in the unforgettable chapter in *Things as They Are* titled "Muzza." I think of the awful hardships, the drudgery and prevailing loneliness that permeate his powerful, deceptively simple story from the Great Depression, *Far from Cibola*.

The failings of humankind are all within his large vision.

In spirit or tone he can be brisk, funny, biblical, arch, down-to-earth. And elegant. I know of no more elegant American writer.

Here is one line from *No Quarter Given*. He is describing two characters from the New York theater:

"They arose, and folded their pride or their furies around themselves, and went, each the axis upon which a world spun."

He knows just how to give us a character, or an age, with a single deftly chosen quote, as when he tells of the brutal Spanish conqueror dying of his wounds who, when asked where he hurt the most, replied, "In my soul."

Or Winfield Scott's comment on Zachary Taylor that "few men ever had a more comfortable, labor-saving contempt for learning of any kind."

Greatest of all, it seems to me, is his gift of empathy. He can take us into other times, into the hearts of other men and women, because he can himself enter into their lives so fully, not just as an actor playing a part, but as a fellow human being.

"My hope is always to make the reader feel what happened, rather than telling him the facts," he says.

He talks also of the gratification that comes with submerging one's self in a large purpose. His work is a calling, and he gives himself to it entirely. In all, one senses it is an act of devotion. Certainly, the moral choices at the center of life are central to nearly everything he writes. He is, all in all, a profoundly moral writer, and though his religious views are never paraded, never made obtrusive, he is plainly a man, like those Spaniards he has written of, for whom faith is a condition of his very being.

"The mystery which lies at the heart of literature," he has written, "must be related to love—love of subject, love of the act of work, love of the human mind and its desire to be informed. . . ."

IN THE CRAFT OF history, he has made his own way, self-taught. He is proof of Henry Steele Commager's observation that all the great historians are self-taught.

Like Parkman and Prescott, he has raised the writing of history to the level of literature.

"The true artist," he says, "is never afraid of anything, including the glories of the past."

The writer of history, he says, "must possess a low threshold of boredom—at all costs he must write in such a way as to save himself from being bored either by his own material or his own manner."

"Historical writing which is not literature," he says, "is subject to oblivion."

Of the art of fiction, inventive writing, as he likes to call it, he has this to say:

"He who fears to be out of mode does not deserve to belong to himself. Every imaginative production must contain some element of risk." (Paul once mentioned to me his disappointment in rereading a certain well-known American classic, and when I asked why, he said because the author showed no nerve.)

"The most valuable writers," he says, "are those in whom we find not themselves, or our selves, or the fugitive era of their lifetime, but the common vision of all times."

ACCURACY AND IMAGINATION

Tribute to Herman Wouk

Remarks delivered in 1995 at the Library of Congress at an event celebrating novelist Herman Wouk's eightieth birthday.

Anyone who writes history and leaves out feeling isn't writing history. Maybe we can never truly know anything without feeling.

I see no rigid distinction between the art of the historic novelist and the art of the historian, the best of the historians. The characters in Herman Wouk's *The Winds of War* and *War and Remembrance* are real because they are in our hearts. I have a dream of a temporary exhibit in Statuary Hall at the Capitol—it might only be for a day—with the statues of imaginary figures of American history, of Huckleberry Finn and Jim, Frank Skeffington, Scarlett O'Hara, Willy Loman, and Natalie Jastrow and her uncle, and Captain Queeg, and Willie Keith. I imagine the pleasure on the faces of the crowds on seeing them there.

Every summer, hundreds of people go by bus to see a plain grave on the Nebraska prairie of a woman named Anna Pavelka. She was no one of historic consequence, not in the usual sense, but her life was the inspiration for Willa Cather's *My Ántonia*. Cather's transforming art made her forever part of Nebraska, as much a part of our America as are our mountains and rivers.

In his wonderful journal, the French painter Delacroix writes, "What I demand is accuracy for the sake of imagination." That says it, it seems to me. The same holds for historians and novelists, biographers and novelists: What we demand is accuracy for the sake of imagination.

In the essays by Armin von Roon, the fictitious German historian in *The Winds of War* and *War and Remembrance*, we find some of the most vivid history I've ever read by anyone. It is written with spirit and authority by someone who has soaked it all up. Mr. Wouk just said that in order to understand the scenes in this film, in order to understand the reality of this unimaginable tragedy of our time—unimaginable crime of our time—it must be seen in the frame of when it happened.

Last week I went to Union College in Schenectady, New York—one of our best small colleges—with Tom Brokaw to talk about World War II with a group of students who were taking a course on the Holocaust. Though at first a bit intimidated by the television paraphernalia and a little starstruck by the presence of Tom Brokaw, these bright, very attractive young Americans began to loosen up, and it soon became apparent that while they knew a great deal about the Holocaust, they were very vague about World War II. It did not surprise me. Teaching a seminar the year before at Dartmouth, I found that among my students, twenty-five seniors majoring in history, none knew who George Marshall was.

It is sad but true that we are raising a generation of young Americans who are to a large degree historically illiterate. Professors on the right, professors on the left, assault or defend political correctness. Charges and countercharges are made about "thought police" and McCarthyism on campus. Meantime, as reported by *The Boston Globe*, 40 percent of the students haven't the least idea who Joe McCarthy was.

On a flight from Hawaii to San Francisco, I began chatting with a young woman sitting beside me. She told me she was a physician. She had attended a well-known university in the South, then went on to medical school. She was about thirty-five or forty, I would guess. When she asked me what I did, I told her I write history and biography. She said immediately that she had no interest in history. I asked why not. "Because you never know what's true and what isn't true," she said. I asked what she meant. She said, "Well, you know, it all depends on who's writing it." I asked for an example.

"Well, World War II."

I asked, "You think maybe it didn't happen?"

"No, no, not that."

"Then, what?"

"The Holocaust," she said.

She did not believe it had happened. And she was not someone who had been denied education, or books, or who lived in some remote part of the country and knew nothing of the world.

As writers, whether of history, biography, fiction, we must cope with two of the most absorbing of all mysteries: time and human nature.

Years ago I read a book that changed my life, a collection of interviews published in *The Paris Review* called *Writers at Work*, in which there was a marvelous interview with Thornton Wilder. He talked about the difficulty of writing about the past in a way that does not rob events of their character of having occurred in freedom. How to convey the reality that nothing ever had to happen the way it did and that no one ever knew how things would turn out? Now the great artists, of course, and our distinguished novelist, Mr. Wouk, is one of them, do this superbly.

I write narrative history because I love the pull and power of a story and particularly plots driven by character. I also use the narrative form because I think that intellectually it is the most honest way. The imposing advantage of hindsight only comes afterward. History from the mountaintop may take in the large view, but it can also be a kind of looking down on the people of other times. We know so much they didn't know, including, most importantly, how it came out.

I am often asked if I am working on a book, and I say I am. But what

I really feel is that I'm working *in* a book, inside that other time as best I can, and inside the shoes, the skins of the principals.

What were they like? What was it like to have been alive then in their vanished world? A very distinguished historian, biographer, and novelist, the late Paul Horgan, said the capacity every historian or biographer needs especially is empathy.

I must tell you, this is a great moment for me because it's not often that I can be in the same room with three of my heroes: Herman Wouk, Sol Linowitz, and Dan Boorstin, each of whom in his way has helped me in my work. Herman Wouk opened up the possibilities in the drama of history, written from the inside. Sol Linowitz let me see history in the making close-up during the controversy over the Panama Canal treaties. Dan Boorstin, in his work and in conversation, has shown the role of ideas in history and the high level of understanding a writer-biographer can bring to a subject.

To read Herman Wouk is like watching a great athlete. And often, as with great athletes, it's the little moves one admires most. In *War and Remembrance*, a minor character, a tail gunner on the Dauntless plane, is introduced as a gloomy Kentucky mountain boy named Cornett. I don't know how much time any of you have spent with Kentucky mountain people, but *gloomy* is just the word for a good many and Cornett a very Kentucky mountain name. The combination gives perfect authenticity to a minor character who to a lesser writer wouldn't have been worth taking any pains over.

Herman Wouk's handling of details is never as the bad historical novelists do, which is to trowel it all on, the so-called color, the costumes, and the like. The historic detail is intrinsic to the work. And, of course, he sweeps you up in the story, and off you go.

I'm particularly indebted to Mr. Wouk for two personal reasons. I worked one summer vacation from college in a Pittsburgh envelope factory, a job I hated, but every night I came home to *The Caine Mutiny*, and that marvelous book carried me through.

Then, many years later, after finishing my book about Theodore Roosevelt, I was casting about for an idea for the next project. My editor suggested a biography of Franklin Roosevelt. I thought not. I'd just spent four years with the Roosevelts and felt ready for a different kind of protagonist, a different kind of America. And further, I said offhand, if I were ever to write a book about a twentieth-century president, it wouldn't be Franklin Roosevelt. It would be Harry Truman.

I'm still not sure why I said that. I had never before thought of writing a book about Harry Truman. But I went to Missouri and saw what a wealth of material there was at the Truman Library, and on the way home again, mulling it over, I began thinking of Truman's life as a kind of allegory. He was Harry True-man, from a place called Independence, and his journey in life reflected so much about American life in his time. He grew up in a small town when small-town life was the heart of American life. He worked as a farmer in what is now known as the golden era of American agriculture. He went off to the First World War in France, as did his whole generation. Afterward, as a haberdasher, he got wiped out by the depression that swept the Middle West in advance of the Great Depression, and from there he stepped into politics as part of the Pendergast organization, just as the big-city machines were approaching their heyday. Then came the Depression and the New Deal, and off he went to Washington as Senator Truman. And I thought to myself, it's very like Pug Henry—Victor Henry—who in *The Winds of War* and *War and Remembrance* is always turning up exactly where you'd like him to be, so that you can be there with him. And I realized, that's my book! Truman was the story I wanted to write.

So from the bottom of my heart, I thank you, Mr. Wouk.

Because of the works of Herman Wouk, we understand our time as we would not without him. Especially because of *War and Remembrance* and *The Winds of War* and *The Caine Mutiny*, future generations will come to know—and will *feel*—the human reality of World War II in a way not otherwise possible. Never the kind of historian who writes only for other historians, this immensely gifted storyteller has brought our twentieth-century history to life as only a very few novelists have been able to do, and we are all his beneficiaries.

One final word that hasn't been used today. Along with so much else, the man we honor is a patriot.

In *War and Remembrance*, there's a point where Victor Henry, commenting on Admiral Nimitz and his brilliant command at Midway, quotes the navy adage: "If it works, you're a hero. If it doesn't work, you're a bum."

Mr. Wouk, you're no bum.

FAVORITE AND INFLUENTIAL BOOKS

DMcC liked to make lists. He handwrote or typed lists of all kinds— people he admired, future tuitions he would have to pay, old-time sayings, memorable restaurants, places he wanted to visit, places he never wanted to go again.

The first list was in his files, dated February 5, 2019. The second is a composite of several book lists.

Ben and Me by Robert Lawson

I read this wonderful account of the "real" Benjamin Franklin, as told by a mouse that lived in Ben's hat, when I was about ten, and suddenly history came to life in a way I loved. I've been strongly recommending it ever since.

A Night to Remember by Walter Lord

This superb book entered my life not long after I had finished college and started work in publishing in New York. It is a story powerfully told, and not long after reading it, I met and got to know Walter, from whom I learned a lot about how he went about the process of writing as he did, which was of great help to me.

The Trees by Conrad Richter
A superb example, like *Ben and Me*, of historical fiction at its best, and it set me to reading all of Richter's work and a subsequent friendship with him. And again, as with Walter Lord, much that I learned from him about the art of storytelling shaped my own development as a writer.

The Proud Tower by Barbara Tuchman
The admiration I've long had for all of Tuchman's books could not be greater, but it was at the time I was writing my own first book, *The Johnstown Flood*, that *The Proud Tower*, a portrait of the world from 1890 to 1914, was first published, and I turned to it again and again for inspiration.

A Stillness at Appomattox by Bruce Catton
A landmark publishing event, a book that set much of the country reading about the Civil War for the first time and certainly awakened my interest in the subject as nothing had until then.

The Killer Angels by Michael Shaara
Another example of historical fiction that works its magic in its way and brings the reader into the human reality of history in brilliant fashion.

The Autocrat of the Breakfast-Table by Oliver Wendell Holmes Sr.
An autobiography by one of the most interesting and amusing Americans of the nineteenth century and a reminder that history is not about politics and war only.

Other Favorite Books over the Years

The Little Engine That Could by Watty Piper
Horton Hatches the Egg by Dr. Seuss

HISTORY MATTERS

Paddle-to-the-Sea by Holling C. Holling
The Road from Coorain by Jill Ker Conway
Angela's Ashes by Frank McCourt
Silent Spring by Rachel Carson
The Expedition of Humphry Clinker by Tobias Smollett
The Rise and Fall of the Third Reich by William Shirer
The Warden by Anthony Trollope
Patrick O'Brian
A Tale of Two Cities by Charles Dickens
Burr by Gore Vidal
Kenneth Roberts
Angle of Repose by Wallace Stegner
The Gay Place by Billy Lee Brammer
Flannery O'Connor
Willa Cather

A BOOK ON EVERY BED

Beginning in the early 1990s, until the end of his life, the requests for DMcC's time and attention arrived like an ongoing avalanche. It was relentless. He vacillated between frustration at the onslaught and his natural, enthusiastic inclination to take part in everything. It was often my job to deliver the news of a decline and then remind him, sometimes over and over, that we said no, and no was what he meant.

Occasionally, a request would arrive that would delight him. This one came from the Boston bookstore Waterstone's in 1995: Would he write something, anything, for their Christmas newsletter?

Christmas and books have been tied up together in my mind for so long I'm not altogether sure whether it's because of my feelings for Christmas that I love books, or if it's the other way around. In any event, as my family knows, books are what I give at Christmas, and books are what I hope to be receiving come the magic morning; and as all in my family—children, grandchildren—also know, this goes back to a Christmas tradition started by my mother and father in the home where I grew up in Pittsburgh.

Every Christmas Eve, we McCullough children—four boys—went to bed knowing what to expect the next morning. Well before our father had put on his ancient, faded Indian blanket bathrobe to lead the march downstairs to who knew what Christmas bounty in the living room, even at the very moment of opening our eyes, we would each find a first present at the foot of our bed.

It was always beautifully wrapped, with ribbon and bow, and it was always a book. And thus did the biggest day of the year begin at 549 Glen Arden Drive.

Now, with this glorious moment went an implicit understanding that once having opened our books, we four, each on his own, would spend time enjoying it to himself—*quietly*, that is—and thereby grant mother and father more sleep. And in time to come, having become a parent, I would see in this, as in other things, the wisdom of my mother and father.

So my five children, too, were to awaken Christmas mornings to find books at the foot of their beds, and my wife and I, too, having been up most of the night wrapping presents, struggling to assemble this or that impossible-to-assemble game or toy, would enjoy a blessed extra half hour or so of morning sleep.

But how can I describe the pleasure with which I chose those books? Or the fun of stealing in and out of dark rooms to put them at the foot of five beds?

Often they were the same titles as those from my own childhood, wonderful books still in print and that I could happily dip into before the wrapping paper went on: *The Little Engine That Could*, *Horton Hatches the Egg*, *Mr. Popper's Penguins*, *Paddle-to-the-Sea*, *The Call of the Wild*. . . . Oh how I loved *Mr. Popper's Penguins*, and still do.

But of course there were lots of new titles as well, many more new titles, and no less wonderful stories year by year. My sons remember receiving books by Farley Mowat and Ray Bradbury, for example. I remember one Christmas Eve starting to look through Elizabeth Speare's *The Witch of Blackbird Pond*, a choice for our oldest daughter, and finding myself so caught up that I read nearly the whole book.

But try it yourself is my recommendation—to all parents, grandparents, aunts, uncles, to anyone who loves a child, a book at the foot of the bed for Christmas morning.

PART FOUR

ON WRITING

THE GOOD, HARD WORK OF WRITING WELL

Remarks delivered at a conference about writing at Dartmouth College in 2012.

We speak a language that isn't ours. It's been handed down to us with a tradition of expression and power that is well worth a lifetime of study, and particularly for those for whom writing is a way of life. I love what I do. I love every day of it. Happiness—true happiness—is not to be found in vacations or the like. It's to be found in the love of learning and doing what you really want to get up and get to each day. And yes, happiness is to be found in writing, because, for one thing, writing focuses the brain like nothing else.

Writing is hard work, make no mistake, but that's what makes it so captivating. Writing is a chance to enlarge life. You learn to write by writing, just as you learn to paint by painting or to play the piano by playing the piano. As an old piano teacher liked to say to her students, "I hear all the notes, but I hear no music."

Write to make music. Don't just pound out notes. We are all trying to make music.

There is no one way to write. It's what works for you. Very often, you won't know what works for you until you've done those four pages a day maybe for four or five years.

It's when you begin writing that you begin to see how much more you need to know. There are so many people who have such interesting lives that have yet to be discovered and shared with others. Leads are everywhere. There's never going to be a shortage of ideas out there in the world. So share your ideas with others! Tell others what you're working on. You never know from whence or from whom that "trunk in the attic full of historic treasures" will come.

Do research as you write, not just before you write. Do research from the beginning to the end—and then you might even want to keep researching after you're done.

Go where things happened and walk the walk. Go to the Kentucky coal town or the boulevards of Paris if that's what is needed. If you're writing about jungles of Panama, go there.

Remember the five senses. What was the smell in the air? How did the light fall? What were the sounds of early morning?

Charles Dickens's great admonition to writers was "Make me see."

My wonderful old high school English teacher, Lowell Innes, used to say over and over, "Don't tell me. Show me."

Take drawing lessons. Try painting. It will teach you how to look at things as you never have. Learn to observe closely. *And then take time to think about it.*

And read a lot. Don't just read what others have written, read what they read, too. This is particularly important when trying to understand or portray life in a time very different from our own. When the HBO producers asked me for advice about preparing the John Adams miniseries. I told them, "Please don't let it become a costume pageant. Life then must be shown to be as difficult and often unpleasant as it truly was, and please don't violate the vocabulary of the eighteenth century." Writers ought not violate the vocabulary of other times any more than distort the facts.

One of the most obvious differences between writing history and fic-

HISTORY MATTERS

tion is the inability to create dialogue. When writing history, you can't invent what people said. You have to go find what they said—in letters, diaries, court testimony, and so forth. And there's plenty to be found.

Writing history is like working on a detective case. And once on the case, you want to know more and more and more. Follow your curiosity. Our curiosity is what separates us from the cabbages. And curiosity, happily, is accelerative like gravity.

The job is to bring historical characters to life. Your subjects were real human beings, after all. Show their strengths, their failings. And remember you're writing about people who didn't know how things would turn out, any more than we do.

In a very real way, there is no such thing as the past. And no one ever lived in the past. They were living in the present, their present, much like we do. History is human, let us remember. "When in the course of human events . . ." The key word there is *human*.

There is every chance to be as creative writing history as there is writing fiction. There are many stories too long untold, and no shortage of topics to pursue. Things often happen in real life that if you were to put them in a novel, people would say, "That's too unrealistic!" even though it was what actually happened. I would be very happy writing fiction. Real life, though, is so often so much more remarkable.

I'm not an expert. I don't ever want to be an expert. Experts supposedly have all the answers. I prefer having questions. If I knew all about the subject, I wouldn't want to write a book about it. I want the project to be a journey, an adventure.

I've never wanted to work by an outline. It would be like painting by the numbers.

I try to write the kind of book that I would like to read.

When talking with some of my academic friends about a project I'm working on, they will often ask about my theme. So I make something up. In reality, I have no idea what the theme is. That's one of the reasons I'm writing the book—to find out what the theme is. I've never undertaken a book on a subject I know all about. The great pull of a project is the thought of how much I'm going to learn.

I don't think one should write to tell people what you want them to think. I want readers to draw their own conclusions from the story I have to tell.

It's part of our human nature to want to know something about what happened before we appeared on the scene. "Once upon a time, long, long ago" are ever magic words. We've survived as a species for thousands of years by passing on what subsequent generations need to know about life through the vehicle of story. We need stories. We have an old, old story hunger, thank heaven.

AND NOW, FROM MY own experience, here is some practical advice about writing:

Don't fool around about beginning what you have to say. Don't sit tapping your foot for a paragraph or two. Get right on with it, get up and dance. But remember, beginnings are crucial! They set the direction and tone.

Let your characters speak for themselves as often as possible.

Write for the ear as well as the eye. Read what you've written aloud, or have someone read it to you. And listen closely. You'll hear mistakes you don't see.

Put what you've written on the shelf for a while and then read it again. Very often you'll see ways to make it better that have eluded you.

Rewrite, rewrite, and rewrite. When asked if I'm a writer, I think sometimes I should say, "No, I'm a rewriter."

Read good writers and especially while working on a project. I crave the release that comes with reading a great novel or great poetry. Try reading geographically or across time. Read everything good that you can get your hands on. Read Penelope Lively and Billy Collins. Read the letters of Flannery O'Connor. Read the murder mysteries of Ruth Rendell. Reading good writers is one of the greatest pleasures in life, but it's also a professional necessity. You have to keep the mind in shape.

History should not ever be dull; it should never be made boring by boring teachers or boring writers. We are raising generations of young Americans who, by and large, are historically illiterate. And that has to change. There is no better way to understand who we are and why we are the way we are and where we may be heading than by reading history from the hands of good writers. I can't imagine a world without books.

A BIT OF HISTORY ABOUT MY TYPEWRITER

DMcC wrote every one of his twelve books on the same typewriter, bought secondhand. He pounded away on it, year after year, decade after decade, typing using just four fingers. When the subject of his typewriter came up, and a child was in earshot, often he would open his eyes wide, lower his voice, and say, "Sometimes I wonder if maybe the typewriter is *writing the books!"*

In 2009, he wrote this essay to accompany a small replica edition of his Royal Standard.

I bought it secondhand in White Plains, New York, back in 1965, at a store called Central Office Equipment on the Post Road that sold typewriters and adding machines.

It was a Royal Standard upright typewriter manufactured in the USA in 1940 or '41. So it was already about twenty-five years old. I've no record of who owned it before or what I paid for it. Maybe it was as much as twenty-five dollars, but then, it was in perfect condition. And *beautiful,* all black with touches of chrome, fully nine inches tall, and good and heavy, and I liked that.

Though I had owned a portable Royal typewriter since college, I now needed the kind I had been using at writing jobs in New York and

Washington. I was about to embark on my first try at a book of my own, working at home at night and on weekends, and I wanted a solid, dependable machine built for serious business.

And oh yes, it had those old-style round keys with little, slightly dished glass covers that feel so good to the touch, which the later model Royal that I used on my day jobs no longer featured.

I rolled a sheet of paper into it there on the counter at the store on the Post Road and had only to type a few words to know I had found the perfect thing.

So home I went in White Plains with my proud new possession, and to work I went on chapter one of what would be *The Johnstown Flood*. A drawing done by Melissa McCullough shows her father and his Royal hard at it on what must have been some of the first pages. Melissa had just turned ten.

More than forty years later, I'm still at it and on the same old Royal. It has been my sturdy tool-of-the-trade through every book I've written. I can't imagine the quantity of words that has meant, since to get things right, to make things clearer, to tighten and sharpen, and put some life into it, I write just about everything many times over. It must add up to the equivalent of five hundred thousand miles on the old machine at the least.

More than forty years in service, and *there's nothing wrong with it!*

Of course, I take it for full servicing and tuning up after each project, and I thank my (and its) lucky stars that my friend and neighbor on Martha's Vineyard Dennis daRosa and his technicians at daRosa Corporation have seen to it all these years that everything's done right and kept a ready supply of ribbons in stock. Yes, you can still get ribbons!

I'VE ALWAYS LOVED MAKING things with my hands. It's often when I'm happiest, and that's the feeling I have working at my typewriter. I never learned to type as one is supposed to, but I go at a pretty good clip. It's long since become perfectly natural. It's what I do, and I enjoy doing it.

I love the way the bell rings every time I swing the carriage lever. I like changing ribbons. I like popping the lid with the white-on-black Royal emblem on it, and dusting off the keys inside with a little black bristle brush made for the purpose.

None of this may have any appeal to most people, but that's all right. There are others who understand what I mean. William Manchester was one. We talked often in years past of the pleasures of a typewriter. Another is Tom Hanks, whose collection of vintage typewriters is not only wondrously extensive but the sign of a man with appreciation for the finer things in life.

So on my Royal and I go with another book, this the ninth, and happily. Nor have I any thought of making changes. Who knows, maybe after all, *it's* writing the books!

READING AND WRITING

A Recommended Reading List

DMcC loved the Library of Congress and the National Book Festival. He loved to talk about books, and he always welcomed the chance to talk about writing. He delivered these remarks at the National Book Festival in 2002.

History, poetry, biography, fiction are not disconnected. And always, always we're interested in beginnings. And if you write books, whether it's history, biography, autobiography, fiction, how do you begin is the crucial question. I love beginnings. I love the beginning of books. I love the beginning of *All the King's Men* with Robert Penn Warren's description of Highway 58 in the night. I love the beginning of a book called *Reveille in Washington* by Margaret Leech, which won the Pulitzer Prize years ago and was one of those books that I read early, after finishing college, that I know helped to set my aspirations, if not the course of my life.

Now imagine if you're Mrs. Leech and you're sitting down to write a book about Washington during the Civil War—about the generals, the cabinet, and, of course, Abraham Lincoln, and all that was going on within the city and just outside the city where much of the war was being fought. How are you going to begin? Where are you going to begin? What tone are you going to set? These are all questions you have to ask.

When I was a young boy, we used to spend summers in the Laurel Mountains of western Pennsylvania. And one day my older brother said to me, let's go climb the mountain that was out in front of the house. So we set off, and it was all woods. And we climbed to the top of the mountain. And then we got up into a tree and we looked back and we could see our house—five, seven miles in the distance. It was starting to get late in the afternoon—night was coming on—and we had to start back. My brother said to me and my younger brother, the three of us, it's very important how we start out, because if we get two or three feet off up here, we'll be two or three *miles* off when we get home. He was a big guy. He had had some geometry, you see.

But that image of starting off in the wrong direction and therefore winding up *way* off course has never left me. And it's absolutely essential in the beginning of a book. Where does it begin? How does it begin? What's the spirit of the beginning? What questions does it ask? What pieces of information does it supply which will be of some significance later on?

Now, there have been endless numbers of dry beginnings to works of history and biography. You could have all the facts correct and miss the truth. Just as you can have some of the facts wrong and hit the truth on the head. You have to have the notes *and* the music. And in Margaret Leech's very opening, you can feel that she is on an interesting track, and this is going to be a book about human beings.

She starts off with a description of the aged Winfield Scott, who is to be the commander, at least initially, of the Union forces—the forces of the United States of America at the start of the Civil War.

> That winter the old General moved from the rooms he had rented from the free mulatto, Wormley, in I Street to Cruchet's at Sixth and D Streets. His new quarters, situated on the ground floor—a spacious bedroom, with a private dining-room adjoining—were

convenient for a man who walked slowly and with pain; and Cruchet, a French caterer, was one of the best cooks in Washington. In spite of nearly seventy-five years and his increasing infirmities, the General was addicted to the pleasures of the table. Before his six o'clock dinner, his black body servant brought out the wines and the liqueurs, setting the bottles of claret to warm before the fire. The old man had refined his palate in the best restaurants in Paris; and woodcock, English snipe, poulard, capon, and *tête de veau en tortue* were among the dishes he fancied. He liked, too, canvasback duck, and the hams of his native Virginia. Yet nothing, to his taste, equaled the delicacy he called "tarrapin." He would hold forth on the correct method of preparing it: "No flour, sir—not a grain." His military secretary could saturninely foresee that moment, when, leaning his left elbow on the table and holding six inches above his plate a fork laden with the succulent tortoise, he would announce, "The best food vouchsafed by Providence to man," before hurrying the fork to his lips.

One of the reasons I love that beginning is because most biographers and historians never give their subjects, their protagonists, a chance to eat. They never feed them. Watch that the next time you read a biography. Did they ever get a chance to eat? Did they ever get a chance to do nothing? Did they ever get a chance to just sort of kick back their heels and be comfortable with old friends and not play a great part in the drama of their times? Which, of course, is all part of life.

Some people think that there's the history of the nation, or the history of diplomacy, or the history of the presidency, or the history of the Congress, and then there's the history of life. None of those are inseparable from the history of life. What was life like? What were those people like, those human beings who lived in distant times? What were the times like?

There were extraordinary times just as there were extraordinary men and women. Extraordinary times come and go. As do exceptional men and women. Exceptional presidents. And one thing to remember about exceptional presidents—it can't be said too often—is that they are the exception. We can't expect every president to be exceptional. It doesn't work that way. Life doesn't work that way.

THESE ARE SOME OF the books that have meant a great deal to me—fiction, nonfiction, biography, autobiography. *A Death in the Family* by James Agee. *My Ántonia* by Willa Cather, which I've read several times. *A Tree Grows in Brooklyn* was the first book I ever took out of the public library in Pittsburgh, Pennsylvania. I was probably about ten years old. *Two Years Before the Mast* by Richard Henry Dana, in a Modern Library edition, which probably cost about fifty cents, I purchased when I was about twelve or fourteen in a bookstore in Pittsburgh. It was the first time I had ever dared to walk into a bookstore on my own and buy a book on my own, a book of my own choice. And I still have it. It's one of my most treasured possessions.

I got through a job one summer working in an envelope factory because I could go home every night after work and read Irwin Shaw's *The Young Lions*, Fitzgerald's *Tender Is the Night*, Herman Wouk's *The Caine Mutiny*, and later on *The Winds of War*. Herman Wouk is a superb writer, and if you read *The Caine Mutiny*, you'll remember Willie Keith always. Willie Keith is a real person in your life. *The Winds of War*, Pug Henry's story, is a story we would all like to experience, too, and he does it for us. And I think some of those historical set pieces, the descriptions of the situation in the War of the World that Mr. Wouk writes and sets in italics every so often through the book, are as well written as any historic descriptions I know.

Turgenev's *Fathers and Sons*. Dickens, of course—all of Dickens. Rosalee and I just last Christmas were in New York. We went over to the Morgan Library, and we saw the original manuscript of *A Christmas Carol*. And if you've never gone to the Morgan Library to see that, go. It's going to send a chill right up your spine. There it is, a little book in Dickens's own hand. I guess if I had to pick my favorite of all of Dickens, it would be *Great Expectations*, but it's a hard choice. Jan de Hartog, a wonderful Dutch writer who just died a few weeks ago, wrote a book called *The Captain* about a tugboat captain on the Murmansk Run, which had a very deep effect on me, as it did to so many others.

Then I began reading political novels. And it's remarkable how few really first-rate political novels we have in our literary body, considering how important politics are, how much we talk about politics, and how much time and money and worry we invest in it. They can be counted maybe on a hand and a half. *Advise and Consent* by Allen Drury. Henry Adams's novel *Democracy*. And the one I keep thinking about again and again—a book called *The Gay Place* by Billy Lee Brammer, a Texan, which is to a very large degree a monologue on Lyndon Johnson—brilliant, brilliant book. Brammer died very shortly after finishing the book. It was a great loss to American letters. If you've not read it, I strongly urge it.

John le Carré's *A Small Town in Germany*—a wonderful book, which has a description of the people working on the research after the war to determine which of the Germans had been Nazis, which of the German businessmen had been Nazis. And in that description, I think he describes as well as anyone ever has the pull, the excitement, the detective-case excitement of historic research. You get on a track, and you want to follow it, want to follow it the whole way. Thomas Flanagan's *The Tenants of Time*, an American writer who wrote beautiful novels about Ireland. *The Tenants of Time* is one of my all-time favorites.

Then I had three writers who befriended me early in my life, all of whom wrote superbly and whose work I treasure. Conrad Richter, whose great trilogy, *The Trees*, *The Fields*, and *The Town*, was very popular years ago. He wrote *The Sea of Grass*. You may remember it was made into a memorable film with Spencer Tracy and Katharine Hepburn. Richter talked to me, as he talked to others, about the power of individual words—the difference between the right word and wrong word—which Mark Twain once described as the difference between lightning and the lightning bug. Paul Horgan—beautiful, beautiful novelist, wonderful biographer. His biography of Archbishop Lamy of Santa Fe is one of the finest biographies I know. And then Thornton Wilder, who I was lucky enough to have at least sat beside on occasion at lunch, and to have talked to several times as an undergraduate in college when Thornton was a fellow of Davenport College at Yale, where I lived.

I love mysteries. I love Martha Grimes. I love Ruth Rendell. I love Ruth Rendell's distinct English depravity. And Elmore Leonard. Elmore Leonard at his best is as good as they get. It's like watching a great tennis player. He knows how to do more on a page with a few lines, a few words, than almost any writer I know.

Among biographies and histories, let's say histories first. Cecil Woodham-Smith's *The Reason Why*. It had a huge effect on me as a young man, as did Frederick Lewis Allen's *Only Yesterday*.

Walter Lord's *A Night to Remember* is an all but perfect example of how to write history without putting in everything you know. And every book is a series of decisions. Every day, writing a book is a series of decisions—what to leave out, how to simplify, how to clarify, how to be clear. That's hard. That's what writing is—it's thinking. And to write well is to think clearly, which is why it's so hard.

Barbara Tuchman's *The Guns of August* and Antoine de Saint-Exupéry's *Wind, Sand and Stars*. I guess I've read that book five times. Harry McPherson wrote a book called *A Political Education*, which I think is the finest book I know about the US Senate, particularly in the time when Lyndon Johnson was in the Senate. It shows what extraordinary characters there were in the Senate then, but also how things work.

Among biographies, I adored Lord David Cecil's *Melbourne*. If you've never seen it or heard of it, get it and read the first page of that book, which is about the stately country homes of the Whigs of England in Melbourne's time, and why they are so vividly expressive of that whole part of English society and how important they were to the course of history. William Manchester's *American Caesar*, his biography of MacArthur. Robert A. Caro's *The Years of Lyndon Johnson*—brilliant. Henri Troyat's *Tolstoy*—again, a wonderful beginning and a wonderful book all the way through. And, of course, Boswell's *Life of Samuel Johnson*.

In autobiography, *The Education of Henry Adams*, which has to be one of the great works ever written by an American. And Benjamin Franklin's autobiography. And I'm particularly fond of the painter Delacroix's *Journal*. It's a very hard book to find, hard to get, but in many libraries. And very well worth reading about what is involved with creativity. There's a line in there that ought to be an emblem that says, "What I demand is accuracy for the sake of imagination." If you start talking about using one's imagination in writing history and biography, there are some people in the world of academia who get very edgy about that, and understandably, I suppose. But what is required is sufficient imagination to project yourself back into that other time, to project yourself back into the lives of those other people, and if possible, inside their skins, and to be empathetic and sympathetic, to understand that just because they didn't know as much as we do, they weren't less bright or less perceptive. And to try to understand how much that we don't even have to think about, particularly if you go back as far, say, as the eighteenth century.

Then there are some books and some poems that I think are essential to understanding our country. Bunyan's *The Pilgrim's Progress* is absolutely one of the essentials because virtually everyone who could, read *The Pilgrim's Progress* through the nineteenth century, along with Shakespeare and the Bible. *Pilgrim's Progress* is really powerful and a source of strength for anyone today, all these hundreds of years later. There's a line in there when Christian, the hero, faces the hideous beast Apollyon and, "with no armor for his back," decides to fight. "The man so bravely play'd the man," Bunyan wrote. "He made the fiend to fly."

In other words, by acting courageous, he made the fiend to fly, and the fiend, of course, is his own fear inside. It's a line that Theodore

Roosevelt knew perfectly and lived by. "By acting as if I was not afraid, I gradually ceased to be afraid," he writes of facing grizzly bears, and bucking horses, and armies in battle.

Somerset Maugham's *The Summing Up* is a book I think every writer should read. It was written long ago, but it has pages and pages of the best kind of advice. And another that I would say is essential, at least it is for me, is a little book by Winston Churchill about *Painting as a Pastime*. It's only twenty-five pages long, and it's wonderful, absolutely wonderful, about the creative urge and the spirit that one has to enter into any creative project. There's another book by a man named Howard Evans, *Life on a Little-Known Planet*, which I adore. Anytime you start feeling that we human beings are the be-all and end-all of creation, read that book. It's all about insects. And it helps keep things in proportion, if anything can.

And then, of course, there's dear old Bartlett's *Familiar Quotations*, which I like to take down in the evening and start reading. Pick out a century and start reading. Pick out the seventeenth century, for example, and start reading. And you'll realize what a rich and not very foreign time that is, when you consider the vibrancy and the majesty of the English language then.

We all—all of us—walk around quoting all these people all the time, particularly the seventeenth- and eighteenth-century writers, and, of course, Shakespeare. We don't know it. We do it every day. If you're "green-eyed with jealousy" or "in a pickle," that's Shakespeare. If you say, "All hell's broke loose," you're quoting Milton's *Paradise Lost*. If you say, "Mum's the word" or "I smell a rat," you're quoting Cervantes's *Don Quixote*. Take out the Bartlett's and just look at how many lines, how many familiar sayings, that you use all the time come from *Don Quixote*, from Cervantes.

One other poem that was so very important for nineteenth-century America was Gray's "Elegy Written in a Country Churchyard," which so many of the people of that day knew by heart. Lincoln, for example; it was his favorite poem. It moved him, it touched him, in a way that nothing else quite had. The sense that we speak words that aren't ours, lines that aren't ours, the feeling that we are carrying on in the vocabulary of the English language, ought to be one of our prime reasons for feeling immense gratitude. This fabulous language we speak, with all its nuances, this vocabulary of ours.

John and Abigail Adams were continuously writing to each other and very often quoting favorite lines without bothering to put quotation marks around them, which was very customary in the eighteenth century, often because they didn't bother much with punctuation or spelling. Jefferson could spell the same word two or three different ways in the same letter, which I admire hugely. Andrew Jackson said he never had much respect for anyone with so little imagination as to be able only to spell a word one way. But also they left quotation marks off because it was a way of paying tribute to the receiver of the letter. I'm not going to put quotation marks around this line because you know the line. It happens again and again.

Take Abigail Adams's famous letter when John is off in Philadelphia and she tells him, reminds him, that when you're working there achieving liberty, "don't forget the ladies." And then she follows with the line "Remember all men would be tyrants if they could." And it's quoted again and again, as Abigail Adams. It's not her line. It's a line from a poem by Daniel Defoe.

When Nathan Hale, a young Nathan Hale from Connecticut, recently graduated from Yale College, was caught by the British in New York and hanged, he is famously to have said as his last words, "I only regret I have but one life to lose for my country." Well, that line isn't his line. It's from a play, from the play *Cato*, which was the most popular play of the day. But imagine you're there and you've been caught and you're going to be hanged, and you're told by these British officers that you have a few minutes to compose yourself and to say your last words. Who in the world could think of any last words in a situation like that? So what does he do? He quotes a kind of scripture. And since it was written by Joseph Addison, who was an Englishman, the Englishmen all knew that line. So I think he was throwing it right back at them, and I think he delivered it this way. "My only regret is that I have but one life to lose for *my* country." That same kind of patriotism, that same kind of commitment to the ideals, applies to *my* country no less than to *yours*.

We are very fortunate, all of us, that we live at a time and in a land where there is such an abundance of choice. We have greater choice in almost everything about life than at any time in all of history. The variety of vocations we can choose, the variety of television channels we can turn on or off, the number of books to read. To walk into a large, present-day bookstore like Barnes & Noble, where there may be one hundred thousand choices, maybe more, and we get to choose. All these different voices, all these different points of view. And we get to choose. Or to go into a great library, where the choice is more vast still; where we can travel in the mind.

HISTORY AND ART

DMcC studied drawing and painting in high school and in college, and for a time he thought he might want to become a professional painter. All of his life, he drew and painted, watercolors mostly, and he enthusiastically encouraged others to pick up a brush or a pencil. Often when he was between books, for a month or two, he would put significant effort into series of pictures, usually with a particular theme—doorways, church steeples, flowers, birds.

In 2004, he delivered the commencement address at the Lyme Academy of Fine Arts.

I am greatly honored to be included in this day of recognition and celebration in this beautiful part of Connecticut in the height of the spring, with lilacs out and those hills having that wonderful soft, green texture that gets that way nowhere else but Connecticut.

In the early spring of 1915, when the world was caught up in the most horrible war in history, until then, Winston Churchill found himself put on the bench, taken out of power. And he was bereft. He was filled, as he said, with great anxiety and no means of relieving it. At a moment, he wrote, "When every fiber of my being was inflamed to action, I was forced to remain a spectator. And then it was that the muse of painting came to my rescue."

In fact, Churchill became quite a good painter. And in the time of the Second World War, he encouraged General Eisenhower to take up painting as a way to sustain the tension of his responsibilities. He told him, "You'd never be able to endure it all, to bear the weight of it. Take up painting." And Ike, as I hope you know, also took up painting. He never achieved the skill and the perfection that Churchill did, but he was quite a good painter. It should come as no surprise to us that one of the greatest figures in history, who, besides being a very great writer and historian, should also have been an avid painter and an exponent of the joys of art. Or that so great a painter as Delacroix, whose work dazzled a dazzling age, should also have delighted in history and wrote knowingly of the challenges of writing and of the historian's art.

Delacroix, writing in his journal in 1850—a generation before Churchill was born—dwelling on the differences between painting and writing. "You see your painting at a single glance," he said. "In your manuscript, you do not even see the whole page, which is to say you cannot embrace it as a whole with your mind." Then he offered these thoughts on writing history, which he saw as still more demanding.

> The task of the historian, it seems to me, is more difficult. He needs sustained attention to a thousand objects at once, and throughout his citations, precise enumerations and the facts which occupy only a realistic position. He has to preserve that warmth which animates the recital and makes it more than an extract from a gazette.

The warmth, as Delacroix said, and the music are vital. History and art. Art and history are ever entwined. Art is history. Art makes history, keeps history alive, often as much or more than the written word. History can be, should be at best, literature, and thus, art.

In my own work, I turn again and again to paintings as a historic source. Portraits, landscapes, cityscapes, marine paintings, battle scenes, sculpture—not to say the sketchbooks and studies that preceded such works. It is in the paintings of John Trumbull, John Singleton Copley, Charles Willson Peale, and Gilbert Stuart that we see the faces of those we call the founders, for example. And that we feel their humanity and their individuality.

But consider the degree to which we are all indebted to succeeding generations of painters and sculptors. For not only information about our history, but for how we feel about who we are and how we came to be the way we are. Whole eras, entire passages in the American experience, are given life and continue to speak to us powerfully down the years.

We have through the century—the turn of the century in New York, the great works of the Ashcan painters. The Armory Show was as much an event in the history of the year 1913 as were the opening of the Woolworth Building or the advent of the income tax. The works of Edward Hopper or of Jackson Pollock are as emblematic of their times, speak to us powerfully of their particular world, as any newspaper headline or politician's memoir. And their names, their names will last far longer in history than will the names of most politicians or war heroes.

One indeed could make a telling chronicle of this whole story of America and hardly have to stray from the works of Connecticut painters alone—from Trumbull to Jim Dine.

And what lives they've led, so many of them. Trumbull was in his time, as I hope you know, a diplomat, a soldier, a founder of the first art gallery in America connected with an institution of higher learning, the Trumbull Gallery at Yale, and an architect and a memoirist. Few Americans have ever contributed so much.

Churchill once wrote that the most industrious, useful people of society may be divided into two categories—those who work with great intensity at their job and for pleasure, for relief, turn to golf or travel or vacation. And then there are those for whom their work and their real joy in life are one and the same—who are thus on vacation every day. And they are the luckiest of all.

May you of the graduating class join their ranks where your work is your joy. And may you take up whatever you do as Hazel Lavery took up the big brush and gave Churchill a lesson in how to address a blank canvas.

"Let those who work lukewarmly be silent," said Delacroix. Read Delacroix. Don't just look at him. Read him. Read his journal—one of the most enthralling books I know. Read Churchill. Read history. Read, read, read. Read Trumbull's memoir. Read the letters of N. C. Wyeth, the magnificent letters of N. C. Wyeth, to his children.

I will close with a line I love. A line that I hope strikes you as right on this beautiful, celebrant day in our troubled world. It's from a very great teacher. A very, very great teacher—Robert Henri. "You should paint like a man coming over the top of a hill singing."

* * *

He lived and worked "like a man coming over the top of a hill singing." David McCullough died on August 7, 2022.

ABOUT THE AUTHORS

David McCullough (1933–2022) twice received the Pulitzer Prize, for *Truman* and *John Adams*, and twice received the National Book Award, for *The Path Between the Seas* and *Mornings on Horseback*. His other acclaimed books include *The Johnstown Flood*, *The Great Bridge*, *Brave Companions*, *1776*, *The Greater Journey*, *The American Spirit*, *The Wright Brothers*, and *The Pioneers*. He was the recipient of numerous honors and awards, including the Presidential Medal of Freedom, the nation's highest civilian award.

Dorie McCullough Lawson is David McCullough's daughter and worked with him for nearly three decades. She is the author of three previous books, including *Posterity: Letters of Great Americans to Their Children*.

Michael Hill is an independent historical researcher who worked with David McCullough for more than thirty years. He is also the author of three previous books, including a biography of Elihu Washburne. He served as a historical consultant for the HBO production of David McCullough's *John Adams*.

Also by
DAVID McCULLOUGH

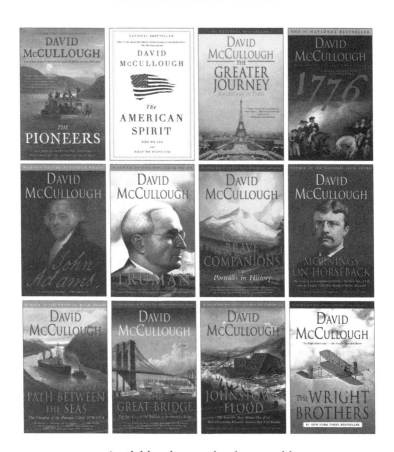

Available wherever books are sold
or at SimonandSchuster.com